O'REILLY®
Strata
Making Data Work

Learn how to turn data into decisions.

From startups to the Fortune 500, smart companies are betting on data-driven insight, seizing the opportunities that are emerging from the convergence of four powerful trends:

- New methods of collecting, managing, and analyzing data

- Cloud computing that offers inexpensive storage and flexible, on-demand computing power for massive data sets

- Visualization techniques that turn complex data into images that tell a compelling story

- Tools that make the power of data available to anyone

Get control over big data and turn it into insight with O'Reilly's Strata offerings. Find the inspiration and information to create new products or revive existing ones, understand customer behavior, and get the data edge.

O'REILLY®

Visit oreilly.com/data to learn more.

Python and HDF5

Andrew Collette

Beijing · Cambridge · Farnham · Köln · Sebastopol · Tokyo

Python and HDF5

by Andrew Collette

Printed in the United States of America.

Published by O'Reilly Media, Inc., 1005 Gravenstein Highway North, Sebastopol, CA 95472.

O'Reilly books may be purchased for educational, business, or sales promotional use. Online editions are also available for most titles (*http://my.safaribooksonline.com*). For more information, contact our corporate/institutional sales department: 800-998-9938 or *corporate@oreilly.com*.

Editors: Meghan Blanchette and Rachel Roumeliotis	**Indexer:** WordCo Indexing Services
Production Editor: Nicole Shelby	**Cover Designer:** Karen Montgomery
Copyeditor: Charles Roumeliotis	**Interior Designer:** David Futato
Proofreader: Rachel Leach	**Illustrator:** Kara Ebrahim

November 2013:   First Edition

Revision History for the First Edition:

2013-10-18:   First release

See *http://oreilly.com/catalog/errata.csp?isbn=9781449367831* for release details.

ISBN: 978-1-449-36783-1

[LSI]

Table of Contents

Preface

Over the past several years, Python has emerged as a credible alternative to scientific analysis environments like IDL or MATLAB. Stable core packages now exist for handling numerical arrays (NumPy), analysis (SciPy), and plotting (matplotlib). A huge selection of more specialized software is also available, reducing the amount of work necessary to write scientific code while also increasing the quality of results.

As Python is increasingly used to handle large numerical datasets, more emphasis has been placed on the use of standard formats for data storage and communication. HDF5, the most recent version of the "Hierarchical Data Format" originally developed at the National Center for Supercomputing Applications (NCSA), has rapidly emerged as the mechanism of choice for storing scientific data in Python. At the same time, many researchers who use (or are interested in using) HDF5 have been drawn to Python for its ease of use and rapid development capabilities.

This book provides an introduction to using HDF5 from Python, and is designed to be useful to anyone with a basic background in Python data analysis. Only familiarity with Python and NumPy is assumed. Special emphasis is placed on the native HDF5 feature set, rather than higher-level abstractions on the Python side, to make the book as useful as possible for creating portable files.

Finally, this book is intended to support both users of Python 2 and Python 3. While the examples are written for Python 2, any differences that may trip you up are noted in the text.

Conventions Used in This Book

The following typographical conventions are used in this book:

Italic
> Indicates new terms, URLs, email addresses, filenames, and file extensions.

Constant width

> Used for program listings, as well as within paragraphs to refer to program elements such as variable or function names, databases, data types, environment variables, statements, and keywords.

Constant width bold

> Shows commands or other text that should be typed literally by the user.

Constant width italic

> Shows text that should be replaced with user-supplied values or by values determined by context.

 This icon signifies a tip, suggestion, or general note.

 This icon indicates a warning or caution.

Using Code Examples

This book is here to help you get your job done. In general, if example code is offered with this book, you may use it in your programs and documentation. You do not need to contact us for permission unless you're reproducing a significant portion of the code. For example, writing a program that uses several chunks of code from this book does not require permission. Selling or distributing a CD-ROM of examples from O'Reilly books does require permission. Answering a question by citing this book and quoting example code does not require permission. Incorporating a significant amount of example code from this book into your product's documentation does require permission.

We appreciate, but do not require, attribution. An attribution usually includes the title, author, publisher, and ISBN. For example: "*Python and HDF5* by Andrew Collette (O'Reilly). Copyright 2014 Andrew Collette, 978-1-449-36783-1."

If you feel your use of code examples falls outside fair use or the permission given above, feel free to contact us at *permissions@oreilly.com*.

Safari® Books Online

 Safari Books Online is an on-demand digital library that delivers expert content in both book and video form from the world's leading authors in technology and business.

Technology professionals, software developers, web designers, and business and creative professionals use Safari Books Online as their primary resource for research, problem solving, learning, and certification training.

Safari Books Online offers a range of product mixes and pricing programs for organizations, government agencies, and individuals. Subscribers have access to thousands of books, training videos, and prepublication manuscripts in one fully searchable database from publishers like O'Reilly Media, Prentice Hall Professional, Addison-Wesley Professional, Microsoft Press, Sams, Que, Peachpit Press, Focal Press, Cisco Press, John Wiley & Sons, Syngress, Morgan Kaufmann, IBM Redbooks, Packt, Adobe Press, FT Press, Apress, Manning, New Riders, McGraw-Hill, Jones & Bartlett, Course Technology, and dozens more. For more information about Safari Books Online, please visit us online.

How to Contact Us

Please address comments and questions concerning this book to the publisher:

O'Reilly Media, Inc.
1005 Gravenstein Highway North
Sebastopol, CA 95472
800-998-9938 (in the United States or Canada)
707-829-0515 (international or local)
707-829-0104 (fax)

We have a web page for this book, where we list errata, examples, and any additional information. You can access this page at *http://oreil.ly/python-HDF5*.

To comment or ask technical questions about this book, send email to *bookques tions@oreilly.com*.

For more information about our books, courses, conferences, and news, see our website at *http://www.oreilly.com*.

Find us on Facebook: *http://facebook.com/oreilly*

Follow us on Twitter: *http://twitter.com/oreillymedia*

Watch us on YouTube: *http://www.youtube.com/oreillymedia*

Acknowledgments

I would like to thank Quincey Koziol, Elena Pourmal, Gerd Heber, and the others at the HDF Group for supporting the use of HDF5 by the Python community. This book benefited greatly from reviewer comments, including those by Eli Bressert and Anthony Scopatz, as well as the dedication and guidance of O'Reilly editor Meghan Blanchette.

Darren Dale and many others deserve thanks for contributing to the h5py project, along with Francesc Alted, Antonio Valentino, and fellow authors of PyTables who first brought the HDF5 and Python worlds together. I would also like to thank Steve Vincena and Walter Gekelman of the UCLA Basic Plasma Science Facility, where I first began working with large-scale scientific datasets.

## CHAPTER 1

Introduction

When I was a graduate student, I had a serious problem: a brand-new dataset, made up of millions of data points collected painstakingly over a full week on a nationally recognized plasma research device, that contained values that were much too small.

About *40 orders of magnitude* too small.

My advisor and I huddled in his office, in front of the shiny new G5 Power Mac that ran our visualization suite, and tried to figure out what was wrong. The data had been acquired correctly from the machine. It looked like the original raw file from the experiment's digitizer was fine. I had written a (very large) script in the IDL programming language on my Thinkpad laptop to turn the raw data into files the visualization tool could use. This in-house format was simplicity itself: just a short fixed-width header and then a binary dump of the floating-point data. Even so, I spent another hour or so writing a program to verify and plot the files on my laptop. They were fine. And yet, when loaded into the visualizer, all the data that looked so beautiful in IDL turned into a featureless, unstructured mush of values all around 10^{-41}.

Finally it came to us: both the digitizer machines and my Thinkpad used the "little-endian" format to represent floating-point numbers, in contrast to the "big-endian" format of the G5 Mac. Raw values written on one machine couldn't be read on the other, and vice versa. I remember thinking *that's so stupid* (among other less polite variations). Learning that this problem was so common that IDL supplied a special routine to deal with it (SWAP_ENDIAN) did not improve my mood.

At the time, I didn't care that much about the details of how my data was stored. This incident and others like it changed my mind. As a scientist, I eventually came to recognize that the choices we make for organizing and storing our data are also choices about communication. Not only do standard, well-designed formats make life easier for individuals (and eliminate silly time-wasters like the "endian" problem), but they make it possible to share data with a global audience.

Python and HDF5

In the Python world, consensus is rapidly converging on Hierarchical Data Format version 5, or "HDF5," as the standard mechanism for storing large quantities of numerical data. As data volumes get larger, organization of data becomes increasingly important; features in HDF5 like named datasets (Chapter 3), hierarchically organized groups (Chapter 5), and user-defined metadata "attributes" (Chapter 6) become essential to the analysis process.

Structured, "self-describing" formats like HDF5 are a natural complement to Python. Two production-ready, feature-rich interface packages exist for HDF5, h5py, and PyTables, along with a number of smaller special-purpose wrappers.

Organizing Data and Metadata

Here's a simple example of how HDF5's structuring capability can help an application. Don't worry too much about the details; later chapters explain both the details of how the file is structured, and how to use the HDF5 API from Python. Consider this a taste of what HDF5 can do for your application. If you want to follow along, you'll need Python 2 with NumPy installed (see Chapter 2).

Suppose we have a NumPy array that represents some data from an experiment:

```
>>> import numpy as np
>>> temperature = np.random.random(1024)
>>> temperature
array([ 0.44149738,  0.7407523 ,  0.44243584, ...,  0.19018119,
        0.64844851,  0.55660748])
```

Let's also imagine that these data points were recorded from a weather station that sampled the temperature, say, every 10 seconds. In order to make sense of the data, we have to record that sampling interval, or "delta-T," somewhere. For now we'll put it in a Python variable:

```
>>> dt = 10.0
```

The data acquisition started at a particular time, which we will also need to record. And of course, we have to know that the data came from Weather Station 15:

```
>>> start_time = 1375204299  # in Unix time
>>> station = 15
```

We could use the built-in NumPy function `np.savez` to store these values on disk. This simple function saves the values as NumPy arrays, packed together in a ZIP file with associated names:

```
>>> np.savez("weather.npz", data=temperature, start_time=start_time, station=
station)
```

We can get the values back from the file with `np.load`:

```
>>> out = np.load("weather.npz")
>>> out["data"]
array([ 0.44149738,  0.7407523 ,  0.44243584, ...,  0.19018119,
        0.64844851,  0.55660748])
>>> out["start_time"]
array(1375204299)
>>> out["station"]
array(15)
```

So far so good. But what if we have more than one quantity per station? Say there's also wind speed data to record?

```
>>> wind = np.random.random(2048)
>>> dt_wind = 5.0    # Wind sampled every 5 seconds
```

And suppose we have multiple stations. We could introduce some kind of naming convention, I suppose: "wind_15" for the wind values from station 15, and things like "dt_wind_15" for the sampling interval. Or we could use multiple files...

In contrast, here's how this application might approach storage with HDF5:

```
>>> import h5py
>>> f = h5py.File("weather.hdf5")
>>> f["/15/temperature"] = temperature
>>> f["/15/temperature"].attrs["dt"] = 10.0
>>> f["/15/temperature"].attrs["start_time"] = 1375204299
>>> f["/15/wind"] = wind
>>> f["/15/wind"].attrs["dt"] = 5.0
---
>>> f["/20/temperature"] = temperature_from_station_20
---

(and so on)
```

This example illustrates two of the "killer features" of HDF5: organization in hierarchical groups and attributes. Groups, like folders in a filesystem, let you store related datasets together. In this case, temperature and wind measurements from the same weather station are stored together under groups named "/15," "/20," etc. Attributes let you attach descriptive metadata *directly to the data it describes*. So if you give this file to a colleague, she can easily discover the information needed to make sense of the data:

```
>>> dataset = f["/15/temperature"]
>>> for key, value in dataset.attrs.iteritems():
...     print "%s: %s" % (key, value)
dt: 10.0
start_time: 1375204299
```

Coping with Large Data Volumes

As a high-level "glue" language, Python is increasingly being used for rapid visualization of big datasets and to coordinate large-scale computations that run in compiled languages like C and FORTRAN. It's now relatively common to deal with datasets hundreds of gigabytes or even terabytes in size; HDF5 itself can scale up to exabytes.

On all but the biggest machines, it's not feasible to load such datasets directly into memory. One of HDF5's greatest strengths is its support for subsetting and partial I/O. For example, let's take the 1024-element "temperature" dataset we created earlier:

```
>>> dataset = f["/15/temperature"]
```

Here, the object named `dataset` is a proxy object representing an HDF5 dataset. It supports array-like slicing operations, which will be familiar to frequent NumPy users:

```
>>> dataset[0:10]
array([ 0.44149738,  0.7407523 ,  0.44243584,  0.3100173 ,  0.04552416,
        0.43933469,  0.28550775,  0.76152561,  0.79451732,  0.32603454])
>>> dataset[0:10:2]
array([ 0.44149738,  0.44243584,  0.04552416,  0.28550775,  0.79451732])
```

Keep in mind that the actual data lives on disk; when slicing is applied to an HDF5 dataset, the appropriate data is found and loaded into memory. Slicing in this fashion leverages the underlying subsetting capabilities of HDF5 and is consequently very fast.

Another great thing about HDF5 is that you have control over how storage is allocated. For example, except for some metadata, a brand new dataset takes *zero* space, and by default bytes are only used on disk to hold the data you actually write.

For example, here's a 2-terabyte dataset you can create on just about any computer:

```
>>> big_dataset = f.create_dataset("big", shape=(1024, 1024, 1024, 512),
dtype='float32')
```

Although no storage is yet allocated, the entire "space" of the dataset is available to us. We can write anywhere in the dataset, and only the bytes on disk necessary to hold the data are used:

```
>>> big_dataset[344, 678, 23, 36] = 42.0
```

When storage is at a premium, you can even use transparent compression on a dataset-by-dataset basis (see Chapter 4):

```
>>> compressed_dataset = f.create_dataset("comp", shape=(1024,), dtype='int32',
compression='gzip')
>>> compressed_dataset[:] = np.arange(1024)
>>> compressed_dataset[:]
array([   0,    1,    2, ..., 1021, 1022, 1023])
```

What Exactly Is HDF5?

HDF5 is a great mechanism for storing *large numerical arrays of homogenous type*, for data models that can be *organized hierarchically* and benefit from tagging of datasets with *arbitrary metadata*.

It's quite different from SQL-style relational databases. HDF5 has quite a few organizational tricks up its sleeve (see Chapter 8, for example), but if you find yourself needing to enforce relationships between values in various tables, or wanting to perform JOINs on your data, a relational database is probably more appropriate. Likewise, for tiny 1D datasets you need to be able to read on machines without HDF5 installed. Text formats like CSV (with all their warts) are a reasonable alternative.

HDF5 is just about perfect if you make minimal use of relational features and have a need for very high performance, partial I/O, hierarchical organization, and arbitrary metadata.

So what, specifically, is "HDF5"? I would argue it consists of three things:

1. A file specification and associated data model.
2. A standard library with API access available from C, C++, Java, Python, and others.
3. A software ecosystem, consisting of both client programs using HDF5 and "analysis platforms" like MATLAB, IDL, and Python.

HDF5: The File

In the preceding brief examples, you saw the three main elements of the HDF5 data model: *datasets*, array-like objects that store your numerical data on disk; *groups*, hierarchical containers that store datasets and other groups; and *attributes*, user-defined bits of metadata that can be attached to datasets (and groups!).

Using these basic abstractions, users can build specific "application formats" that organize data in a method appropriate for the problem domain. For example, our "weather station" code used one group for each station, and separate datasets for each measured parameter, with attributes to hold additional information about what the datasets mean. It's very common for laboratories or other organizations to agree on such a "format-within-a-format" that specifies what arrangement of groups, datasets, and attributes are to be used to store information.

Since HDF5 takes care of all cross-platform issues like endianness, sharing data with other groups becomes a simple matter of manipulating groups, datasets, and attributes to get the desired result. And because the files are *self-describing*, even knowing about the application format isn't usually necessary to get data out of the file. You can simply open the file and explore its contents:

```
>>> f.keys()
[u'15', u'big', u'comp']
>>> f["/15"].keys()
[u'temperature', u'wind']
```

Anyone who has spent hours fiddling with byte-offsets while trying to read "simple" binary formats can appreciate this.

Finally, the low-level byte layout of an HDF5 file on disk is an open specification. There are no mysteries about how it works, in contrast to proprietary binary formats. And although people typically use the library provided by the HDF Group to access files, nothing prevents you from writing your own reader if you want.

HDF5: The Library

The HDF5 file specification and open source library is maintained by the HDF Group (*http://www.hdfgroup.org*), a nonprofit organization headquartered in Champaign, Illinois. Formerly part of the University of Illinois Urbana-Champaign, the HDF Group's primary product is the HDF5 software library.

Written in C, with additional bindings for C++ and Java, this library is what people usually mean when they say "HDF5." Both of the most popular Python interfaces, PyTables and h5py, are designed to use the C library provided by the HDF Group.

One important point to make is that this library is actively maintained, and the developers place a strong emphasis on backwards compatibility. This applies to both the files the library produces and also to programs that use the API. File compatibility is a must for an archival format like HDF5. Such careful attention to API compatibility is the main reason that packages like h5py and PyTables have been able to get traction with many different versions of HDF5 installed in the wild.

You should have confidence when using HDF5 for scientific data storage, including long-term storage. And since both the library and format are open source, your files will be readable even if a meteor takes out Illinois.

HDF5: The Ecosystem

Finally, one aspect that makes HDF5 particularly useful is that you can read and write files from just about every platform. The IDL language has supported HDF5 for years; MATLAB has similar support and now even uses HDF5 as the default format for its ".mat" save files. Bindings are also available for Python, C++, Java, .NET, and LabView, among others. Institutional users include NASA's Earth Observing System, whose "EOS5" format is an application format on top of the HDF5 container, as in the much simpler example earlier. Even the newest version of the competing NetCDF format, NetCDF4, is implemented using HDF5 groups, datasets, and attributes.

Hopefully I've been able to share with you some of the things that make HDF5 so exciting for scientific use. Next, we'll review the basics of how HDF5 works and get started on using it from Python.

## CHAPTER 2

Getting Started

HDF5 Basics

Before we jump into Python code examples, it's useful to take a few minutes to address how HDF5 itself is organized. Figure 2-1 shows a cartoon of the various logical layers involved when using HDF5. Layers shaded in blue are internal to the library itself; layers in green represent software that uses HDF5.

Most client code, including the Python packages h5py and PyTables, uses the native *C API* (HDF5 is itself written in C). As we saw in the introduction, the HDF5 data model consists of three main *public abstractions*: datasets (see Chapter 3), groups (see Chapter 5), and attributes (see Chapter 6)in addition to a system to represent types. The C API (and Python code on top of it) is designed to manipulate these objects.

HDF5 uses a variety of *internal data structures* to represent groups, datasets, and attributes. For example, groups have their entries indexed using structures called "B-trees," which make retrieving and creating group members very fast, even when hundreds of thousands of objects are stored in a group (see "How Groups Are Actually Stored" on page 65). You'll generally only care about these data structures when it comes to performance considerations. For example, when using chunked storage (see Chapter 4), it's important to understand how data is actually organized on disk.

The next two layers have to do with how your data makes its way onto disk. HDF5 objects all live in a 1D logical address space, like in a regular file. However, there's an extra layer between this space and the actual arrangement of bytes on disk. HDF5 *drivers* take care of the mechanics of writing to disk, and in the process can do some amazing things.

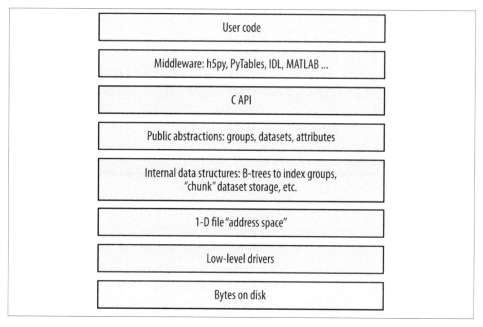

Figure 2-1. The HDF5 library: blue represents components inside the HDF5 library; green represents "client" code that calls into HDF5; gray represents resources provided by the operating system.

For example, the HDF5 `core` driver lets you use files that live entirely in memory and are blazingly fast. The `family` driver lets you split a single file into regularly sized pieces. And the `mpio` driver lets you access the same file from multiple parallel processes, using the Message Passing Interface (MPI) library ("MPI and Parallel HDF5" on page 119). All of this is transparent to code that works at the higher level of groups, datasets, and attributes.

Setting Up

That's enough background material for now. Let's get started with Python! But *which* Python?

Python 2 or Python 3?

A big shift is under way in the Python community. Over the years, Python has accumulated a number of features and misfeatures that have been deemed undesirable. Examples range from packages that use inconsistent naming conventions all the way to deficiencies in how strings are handled. To address these issues, it was decided to launch a new major version (Python 3) that would be freed from the "baggage" of old decisions in the Python 2 line.

Python 2.7, the most recent minor release in the Python series, will also be the *last* 2.X release. Although it will be updated with bug fixes for an extended period of time, new Python code development is now carried out exclusively on the 3.X line. The NumPy package, h5py, PyTables, and many other packages now support Python 3. While (in my opinion) it's a little early to recommend that newcomers start with Python 3, the future is clear.

So at the moment, there are two major versions of Python widely deployed simultaneously. Since most people in the Python community are used to Python 2, the examples in this book are also written for Python 2. For the most part, the differences are minor; for example, on Python 3, the syntax for print is print(foo), instead of print foo. Wherever incompatibilities are likely to occur (mainly with string types and certain dictionary-style methods), these will be noted in the text.

"Porting" code to Python 3 isn't actually that hard; after all, it's still Python. Some of the most valuable features in Python 3 are already present in Python 2.7. A free tool is also available (2to3) that can accomplish most of the mechanical changes, for example changing print statements to print() function calls. Check out the migration guide (and the 2to3 tool) at *http://www.python.org*.

Code Examples

To start with, most of the code examples will follow this form:

```
>>> a = 1.0
>>> print a
1.0
```

Or, since Python prints objects by default, an even simpler form:

```
>>> a
1.0
```

Lines starting with >>> represent input to Python (>>> being the default Python prompt); other lines represent output. Some of the longer examples, where the program output is not shown, omit the >>> in the interest of clarity.

Examples intended to be run from the command line will start with the Unix-style "$" prompt:

```
$ python --version
Python 2.7.3
```

Finally, to avoid cluttering up the examples, most of the code snippets you'll find here will assume that the following packages have been imported:

```
>>> import numpy as np     # Provides array object and data type objects
>>> import h5py            # Provides access to HDF5
```

NumPy

"NumPy" is the standard numerical-array package in the Python world. This book assumes that you have some experience with NumPy (and of course Python itself), including how to use array objects.

Even if you've used NumPy before, it's worth reviewing a few basic facts about how arrays work. First, NumPy arrays all have a fixed data type or "dtype," represented by *dtype objects*. For example, let's create a simple 10-element integer array:

```
>>> arr = np.arange(10)
>>> arr
array([0, 1, 2, 3, 4, 5, 6, 7, 8, 9])
```

The data type of this array is given by `arr.dtype`:

```
>>> arr.dtype
dtype('int32')
```

These dtype objects are how NumPy communicates low-level information about the type of data in memory. For the case of our 10-element array of 4-byte integers (32-bit or "int32" in NumPy lingo), there is a chunk of memory somewhere 40 bytes long that holds the values 0 through 9. Other code that receives the `arr` object can inspect the dtype object to figure out what the memory contents represent.

> The preceding example might print `dtype('int64')` on your system. All this means is that the default integer size available to Python is 64 bits long, instead of 32 bits.

HDF5 uses a very similar type system; every "array" or *dataset* in an HDF5 file has a fixed type represented by a type object. The `h5py` package automatically maps the HDF5 type system onto NumPy dtypes, which among other things makes it easy to interchange data with NumPy. Chapter 3 goes into more detail about this process.

Slicing is another core feature of NumPy. This means accessing *portions* of a NumPy array. For example, to extract the first four elements of our array `arr`:

```
>>> out = arr[0:4]
>>> out
array([0, 1, 2, 3])
```

You can also specify a "stride" or steps between points in the slice:

```
>>> out = arr[0:4:2]
>>> out
array([0, 2])
```

When talking to HDF5, we will borrow this "slicing" syntax to allow loading only portions of a dataset.

In the NumPy world, slicing is implemented in a clever way, which generally creates arrays that *refer* to the data in the original array, rather than independent copies. For example, the preceding out object is likely a "view" onto the original arr array. We can test this:

```
>>> out[:] = 42
>>> out
array([42, 42])
>>> arr
array([42,  1, 42,  3,  4,  5,  6,  7,  8,  9])
```

This means slicing is generally a very fast operation. But you should be careful to explicitly create a copy if you want to modify the resulting array without your changes finding their way back to the original:

```
>>> out2 = arr[0:4:2].copy()
```

 Forgetting to make a copy before modifying a "slice" of the array is a very common mistake, especially for people used to environments like IDL. If you're new to NumPy, be careful!

As we'll see later, thankfully this doesn't apply to slices read from HDF5 datasets. When you read from the file, since the data is on disk, you will always get a copy.

HDF5 and h5py

We'll use the "h5py" package to talk to HDF5. This package contains high-level wrappers for the HDF5 objects of files, groups, datasets, and attributes, as well as extensive low-level wrappers for the HDF5 C data structures and functions. The examples in this book assume h5py version 2.2.0 or later, which you can get at *http://www.h5py.org*.

You should note that h5py is not the only commonly used package for talking to HDF5. PyTables (*http://www.pytables.org*) is a scientific database package based on HDF5 that adds dataset indexing and an additional type system. Since we'll be talking about native HDF5 constructs, we'll stick to h5py, but I strongly recommend you also check out PyTables if those features interest you.

If you're on Linux, it's generally a good idea to install the HDF5 library via your package manager. On Windows, you can download an installer from *http://www.h5py.org*, or use one of the many distributions of Python that include HDF5/h5py, such as PythonXY, Anaconda from Continuum Analytics, or Enthought Python Distribution.

IPython

Apart from NumPy and h5py/HDF5 itself, IPython is a must-have component if you'll be doing extensive analysis or development with Python. At its most basic, IPython is a replacement interpreter shell that adds features like command history and Tab-completion for object attributes. It also has tons of additional features for parallel processing, MATLAB-style "notebook" display of graphs, and more.

The best way to explore the features in this book is with an IPython prompt open, following along with the examples. Tab-completion alone is worth it, because it lets you quickly see the attributes of modules and objects. The h5py package is specifically designed to be "explorable" in this sense. For example, if you want to discover what properties and methods exist on the File object (see "Your First HDF5 File" on page 17), type h5py.File. and bang the Tab key:

```
>>> h5py.File.<TAB>
h5py.File.attrs             h5py.File.get           h5py.File.name
h5py.File.close             h5py.File.id            h5py.File.parent
h5py.File.copy              h5py.File.items         h5py.File.ref
h5py.File.create_dataset    h5py.File.iteritems     h5py.File.require_dataset
h5py.File.create_group      h5py.File.iterkeys      h5py.File.require_group
h5py.File.driver            h5py.File.itervalues    h5py.File.userblock_size
h5py.File.fid               h5py.File.keys          h5py.File.values
h5py.File.file              h5py.File.libver        h5py.File.visit
h5py.File.filename          h5py.File.mode          h5py.File.visititems
h5py.File.flush             h5py.File.mro
```

To get more information on a property or method, use ? after its name:

```
>>> h5py.File.close?
Type:        instancemethod
Base Class: <type 'instancemethod'>
String Form:<unbound method File.close>
Namespace:  Interactive
File:        /usr/local/lib/python2.7/dist-packages/h5py/_hl/files.py
Definition: h5py.File.close(self)
Docstring:  Close the file.  All open objects become invalid
```

 By default, IPython will save the output of your statements in special hidden variables. This is generally OK, but can be surprising if it hangs on to an HDF5 object you thought was discarded, or a big array that eats up memory. You can turn this off by setting the IPython configuration value cache_size to 0. See the docs at *http://ipython.org* for more information.

Timing and Optimization

For performance testing, we'll use the timeit module that ships with Python. Examples using timeit will assume the following import:

```
>>> from timeit import timeit
```

The `timeit` function takes a (string or callable) command to execute, and an optional number of times it should be run. It then prints the total time spent running the command. For example, if we execute the "wait" function `time.sleep` five times:

```
>>> import time
>>> timeit("time.sleep(0.1)", number=5)
0.49967818316434887
```

If you're using IPython, there's a similar built-in "magic" function called `%timeit` that runs the specified statement a few times, and reports the lowest execution time:

```
>>> %timeit time.sleep(0.1)
10 loops, best of 3: 100 ms per loop
```

We'll stick with the regular `timeit` function in this book, in part because it's provided by the Python standard library.

Since people using HDF5 generally deal with large datasets, performance is always a concern. But you'll notice that optimization and benchmarking discussions in this book don't go into great detail about things like cache hits, data conversion rates, and so forth. The design of the h5py package, which this book uses, leaves nearly all of that to HDF5. This way, you benefit from the hundreds of man years of work spent on tuning HDF5 to provide the highest performance possible.

As an application builder, the best thing you can do for performance is to use the API in a sensible way and let HDF5 do its job. Here are some suggestions:

1. Don't optimize anything unless there's a demonstrated performance problem. Then, carefully isolate the misbehaving parts of the code before changing anything.

2. Start with simple, straightforward code that takes advantage of the API features. For example, to iterate over all objects in a file, use the Visitor feature of HDF5 (see "Multilevel Iteration with the Visitor Pattern" on page 68) rather than cobbling together your own approach.

3. Do "algorithmic" improvements first. For example, when writing to a dataset (see Chapter 3), write data in reasonably sized blocks instead of point by point. This lets HDF5 use the filesystem in an intelligent way.

4. Make sure you're using the right data types. For example, if you're running a compute-intensive program that loads floating-point data from a file, make sure that you're not accidentally using double-precision floats in a calculation where single precision would do.

5. Finally, don't hesitate to ask for help on the h5py or NumPy/Scipy mailing lists, Stack Overflow, or other community sites. Lots of people are using NumPy and HDF5 these days, and many performance problems have known solutions. The Python community is very welcoming.

The HDF5 Tools

We'll be creating a number of files in later chapters, and it's nice to have an independent way of seeing what they contain. It's also a good idea to inspect files you create professionally, especially if you'll be using them for archiving or sharing them with colleagues. The earlier you can detect the use of an incorrect data type, for example, the better off you and other users will be.

HDFView

HDFView is a free graphical browser for HDF5 files provided by the HDF Group. It's a little basic, but is written in Java and therefore available on Windows, Linux, and Mac. There's a built-in spreadsheet-like browser for data, and basic plotting capabilities.

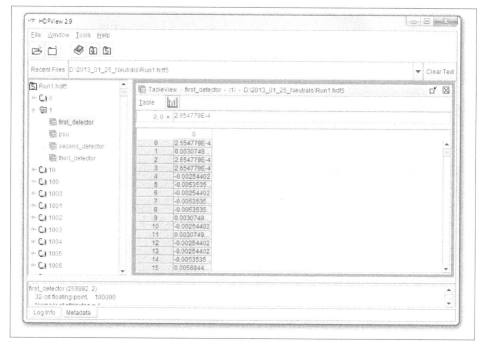

Figure 2-2. HDFView

Figure 2-2 shows the contents of an HDF5 file with multiple groups in the left-hand pane. One group (named "1") is open, showing the datasets it contains; likewise, one dataset is opened, with its contents displayed in the grid view to the right.

HDFView also lets you inspect attributes of datasets and groups, and supports nearly all the data types that HDF5 itself supports, with the exception of certain variable-length structures.

ViTables

Figure 2-3 shows the same HDF5 file open in ViTables, another free graphical browser. It's optimized for dealing with PyTables files, although it can handle generic HDF5 files perfectly well. One major advantage of ViTables is that it comes preinstalled with such Python distributions as PythonXY, so you may already have it.

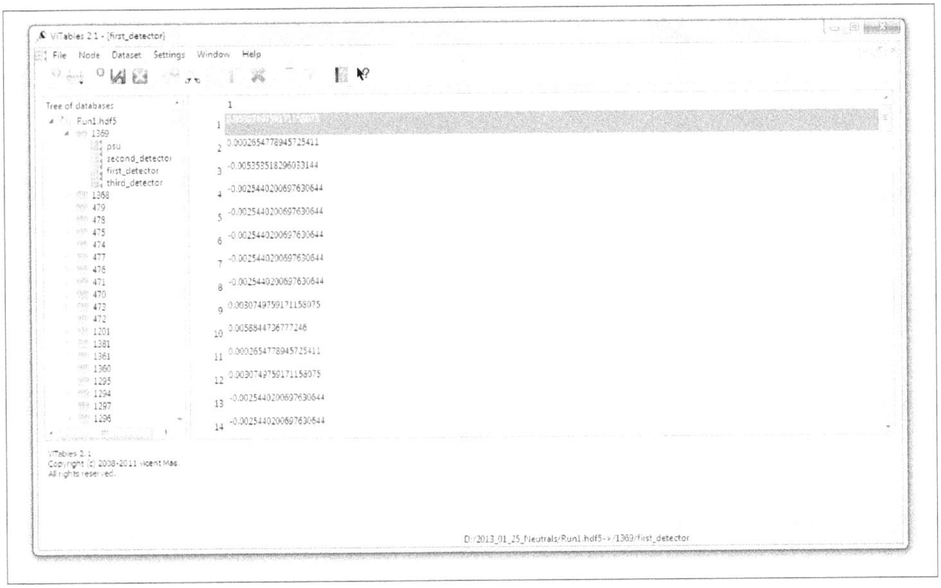

Figure 2-3. ViTables

Command Line Tools

If you're used to the command line, it's definitely worth installing the HDF command-line tools. These are generally available through a package manager; if not, you can get them at www.hdfgroup.org. Windows versions are also available.

The program we'll be using most in this book is called h5ls, which as the name suggests lists the contents of a file. Here's an example, in which h5ls is applied to a file containing a couple of datasets and a group:

```
$ h5ls demo.hdf5
array                    Dataset {10}
group                    Group
scalar                   Dataset {SCALAR}
```

We can get a little more useful information by using the option combo -vlr, which prints extended information and also recursively enters groups:

```
$ h5ls -vlr demo.hdf5
/                          Group
    Location:  1:96
    Links:     1
/array                     Dataset {10/10}
    Location:  1:1400
    Links:     1
    Storage:   40 logical bytes, 40 allocated bytes, 100.00% utilization
    Type:      native int
/group                     Group
    Location:  1:1672
    Links:     1
/group/subarray            Dataset {2/2, 2/2}
    Location:  1:1832
    Links:     1
    Storage:   16 logical bytes, 16 allocated bytes, 100.00% utilization
    Type:      native int
/scalar                    Dataset {SCALAR}
    Location:  1:800
    Links:     1
    Storage:   4 logical bytes, 4 allocated bytes, 100.00% utilization
    Type:      native int
```

That's a little more useful. We can see that the object at /array is of type "native int," and is a 1D array 10 elements long. Likewise, there's a dataset inside the group named group that is 2D, also of type native int.

h5ls is great for inspecting metadata like this. There's also a program called h5dump, which prints data as well, although in a more verbose format:

```
$ h5dump demo.hdf5
HDF5 "demo.hdf5" {
GROUP "/" {
   DATASET "array" {
      DATATYPE  H5T_STD_I32LE
      DATASPACE  SIMPLE { ( 10 ) / ( 10 ) }
      DATA {
      (0): 0, 1, 2, 3, 4, 5, 6, 7, 8, 9
      }
   }
   GROUP "group" {
      DATASET "subarray" {
         DATATYPE  H5T_STD_I32LE
         DATASPACE  SIMPLE { ( 2, 2 ) / ( 2, 2 ) }
         DATA {
         (0,0): 2, 2,
         (1,0): 2, 2
         }
      }
   }
   DATASET "scalar" {
      DATATYPE  H5T_STD_I32LE
```

```
        DATASPACE  SCALAR
        DATA {
        (0): 42
        }
      }
    }
  }
}
```

Your First HDF5 File

Before we get to groups and datasets, let's start by exploring some of the capabilities of the File object, which will be your entry point into the world of HDF5.

Here's the simplest possible program that uses HDF5:

```
>>> f = h5py.File("name.hdf5")
>>> f.close()
```

The File object is your starting point; it has methods that let you create new datasets or groups in the file, as well as more pedestrian properties such as .filename and .mode.

Speaking of .mode, HDF5 files support the same kind of read/write modes as regular Python files:

```
>>> f = h5py.File("name.hdf5", "w")    # New file overwriting any existing file
>>> f = h5py.File("name.hdf5", "r")    # Open read-only (must exist)
>>> f = h5py.File("name.hdf5", "r+")   # Open read-write (must exist)
>>> f = h5py.File("name.hdf5", "a")    # Open read-write (create if doesn't exist)
```

There's one additional HDF5-specific mode, which can save your bacon should you accidentally try to overwrite an existing file:

```
>>> f = h5py.File("name.hdf5", "w-")
```

This will create a new file, but fail if a file of the same name already exists. For example, if you're performing a long-running calculation and don't want to risk overwriting your output file should the script be run twice, you could open the file in w- mode:

```
>>> f = h5py.File("important_file.hdf5", "w-")
>>> f.close()
>>> f = h5py.File("important_file.hdf5", "w-")
IOError: unable to create file (File accessability: Unable to open file)
```

By the way, you're free to use Unicode filenames! Just supply a normal Unicode string and it will transparently work, assuming the underlying operating system supports the UTF-8 encoding:

```
>>> name = u"name_eta_\u03b7"
>>> f = h5py.File(name)
>>> print f.filename
name_eta_η
```

You might wonder what happens if your program crashes with open files. If the program exits with a Python exception, don't worry! The HDF library will automatically close every open file for you when the application exits.

Use as a Context Manager

One of the coolest features introduced in Python 2.6 is support for *context managers*. These are objects with a few special methods called on entry and exit from a block of code, using the `with` statement. The classic example is the built-in Python `file` object:

```
>>> with open("somefile.txt", "w") as f:
...     f.write("Hello!")
```

The preceding code opens a brand-new `file` object, which is available in the code block with the name `f`. When the block exits, the file is automatically closed (even if an exception occurs!).

The `h5py.File` object supports exactly this kind of use. It's a great way to make sure the file is always properly closed, without wrapping everything in `try/except` blocks:

```
>>> with h5py.File("name.hdf5", "w") as f:
...     print f["missing_dataset"]
KeyError: "unable to open object (Symbol table: Can't open object)"
>>> print f
<Closed HDF5 file>
```

File Drivers

File *drivers* sit between the filesystem and the higher-level world of HDF5 groups, datasets, and attributes. They deal with the mechanics of mapping the HDF5 "address space" to an arrangement of bytes on disk. Typically you won't have to worry about which driver is in use, as the default driver works well for most applications.

The great thing about drivers is that once the file is opened, they're totally transparent. You just use the HDF5 library as normal, and the driver takes care of the storage mechanics.

Here are a couple of the more interesting ones, which can be helpful for unusual problems.

core driver

The `core` driver stores your file *entirely in memory*. Obviously there's a limit to how much data you can store, but the trade-off is blazingly fast reads and writes. It's a great choice when you want the speed of memory access, but also want to use the HDF5 structures. To enable, set the `driver` keyword to `"core"`:

```
>>> f = h5py.File("name.hdf5", driver="core")
```

You can also tell HDF5 to create an on-disk "backing store" file, to which the file image is saved when closed:

```
>>> f = h5py.File("name.hdf5", driver="core", backing_store=True)
```

By the way, the `backing_store` keyword will also tell HDF5 to load any existing image from disk when you open the file. So if the entire file will fit in memory, you need to read and write the image only once; things like dataset reads and writes, attribute creation, and so on, don't take any disk I/O at all.

family driver

Sometimes it's convenient to split a file up into multiple images, all of which share a certain maximum size. This feature was originally implemented to support filesystems that couldn't handle file sizes above 2GB.

```
>>> # Split the file into 1-GB chunks
>>> f = h5py.File("family.hdf5", driver="family", memb_size=1024**3)
```

The default for `memb_size` is 2^{31}-1, in keeping with the historical origins of the driver.

mpio driver

This driver is the heart of Parallel HDF5. It lets you access the same file from multiple processes at the same time. You can have dozens or even hundreds of parallel computing processes, all of which share a consistent view of a single file on disk.

Using the `mpio` driver correctly can be tricky. Chapter 9 covers both the details of this driver and best practices for using HDF5 in a parallel environment.

The User Block

One interesting feature of HDF5 is that files may be preceded by arbitrary user data. When a file is opened, the library looks for the HDF5 header at the beginning of the file, then 512 bytes in, then 1024, and so on in powers of 2. Such space at the beginning of the file is called the "user block," and you can store whatever data you want there.

The only restrictions are on the size of the block (powers of 2, and at least 512), and that you shouldn't have the file open in HDF5 when writing to the user block. Here's an example:

```
>>> f = h5py.File("userblock.hdf5", "w", userblock_size=512)
>>> f.userblock_size    # Would be 0 if no user block present
512
>>> f.close()

>>> with open("userblock.hdf5", "rb+") as f:    # Open as regular Python file
...     f.write("a"*512)
```

Let's move on to the first major object in the HDF5 data model, one that will be familiar to users of the NumPy array type: datasets.

## CHAPTER 3

Working with Datasets

Datasets are the central feature of HDF5. You can think of them as NumPy arrays that live on disk. Every dataset in HDF5 has a name, a type, and a shape, and supports random access. Unlike the built-in np.save and friends, there's no need to read and write the entire array as a block; you can use the standard NumPy syntax for slicing to read and write just the parts you want.

Dataset Basics

First, let's create a file so we have somewhere to store our datasets:

```
>>> f = h5py.File("testfile.hdf5")
```

Every dataset in an HDF5 file has a name. Let's see what happens if we just assign a new NumPy array to a name in the file:

```
>>> arr = np.ones((5,2))
>>> f["my dataset"] = arr
>>> dset = f["my dataset"]
>>> dset
<HDF5 dataset "my dataset": shape (5, 2), type "<f8">
```

We put in a NumPy array but got back something else: an instance of the class h5py.Dataset. This is a "proxy" object that lets you read and write to the underlying HDF5 dataset on disk.

Type and Shape

Let's explore the Dataset object. If you're using IPython, type dset. and hit Tab to see the object's attributes; otherwise, do dir(dset). There are a lot, but a few stand out:

```
>>> dset.dtype
dtype('float64')
```

Each dataset has a fixed type that is defined when it's created and can never be changed. HDF5 has a vast, expressive type mechanism that can easily handle the built-in NumPy types, with few exceptions. For this reason, h5py always expresses the type of a dataset using standard NumPy dtype objects.

There's another familiar attribute:

```
>>> dset.shape
(5, 2)
```

A dataset's shape is also defined when it's created, although as we'll see later, it can be changed. Like NumPy arrays, HDF5 datasets can have between zero axes (scalar, shape ()) and 32 axes. Dataset axes can be up to 2^{63}-1 elements long.

Reading and Writing

Datasets wouldn't be that useful if we couldn't get at the underlying data. First, let's see what happens if we just read the entire dataset:

```
>>> out = dset[...]
>>> out
array([[ 1.,   1.],
       [ 1.,   1.],
       [ 1.,   1.],
       [ 1.,   1.],
       [ 1.,   1.]])
>>> type(out)
<type 'numpy.ndarray'>
```

Slicing into a Dataset object returns a NumPy array. Keep in mind what's actually happening when you do this: h5py translates your slicing selection into a portion of the dataset and has HDF5 read the data from disk. In other words, ignoring caching, a slicing operation results in a read or write to disk.

Let's try updating just a portion of the dataset:

```
>>> dset[1:4,1] = 2.0
>>> dset[...]
array([[ 1.,   1.],
       [ 1.,   2.],
       [ 1.,   2.],
       [ 1.,   2.],
       [ 1.,   1.]])
```

Success!

Because Dataset objects are so similar to NumPy arrays, you may be tempted to mix them in with computational code. This may work for a while, but generally causes performance problems as the data is on disk instead of in memory.

Creating Empty Datasets

You don't need to have a NumPy array at the ready to create a dataset. The method create_dataset on our File object can create empty datasets from a shape and type, or even just a shape (in which case the type will be np.float32, native single-precision float):

```
>>> dset = f.create_dataset("test1", (10, 10))
>>> dset
<HDF5 dataset "test1": shape (10, 10), type "<f4">
>>> dset = f.create_dataset("test2", (10, 10), dtype=np.complex64)
>>> dset
<HDF5 dataset "test2": shape (10, 10), type "<c8">
```

HDF5 is smart enough to only allocate as much space on disk as it actually needs to store the data you write. Here's an example: suppose you want to create a 1D dataset that can hold 4 gigabytes worth of data samples from a long-running experiment:

```
>>> dset = f.create_dataset("big dataset", (1024**3,), dtype=np.float32)
```

Now write some data to it. To be fair, we also ask HDF5 to flush its buffers and actually write to disk:

```
>>> dset[0:1024] = np.arange(1024)
>>> f.flush()
```

Looking at the file size on disk:

```
$ ls -lh testfile.hdf5
-rw-r--r-- 1 computer computer 66K Mar  6 21:23 testfile.hdf5
```

Saving Space with Explicit Storage Types

When it comes to types, a few seconds of thought can save you a lot of disk space and also reduce your I/O time. The create_dataset method can accept almost any NumPy dtype for the underlying dataset, and crucially, it doesn't have to exactly match the type of data you later write to the dataset.

Here's an example: one common use for HDF5 is to store numerical floating-point data —for example, time series from digitizers, stock prices, computer simulations—any-where it's necessary to represent "real-world" numbers that aren't integers.

Often, to keep the accuracy of calculations high, 8-byte *double-precision* numbers will be used in memory (NumPy dtype float64), to minimize the effects of rounding error.

However, it's common practice to store these data points on disk as *single-precision*, 4-byte numbers (`float32`), saving a factor of 2 in file size.

Let's suppose we have such a NumPy array called `bigdata`:

```
>>> bigdata = np.ones((100,1000))
>>> bigdata.dtype
dtype('float64')
>>> bigdata.shape
(100, 1000)
```

We could store this in a file by simple assignment, resulting in a double-precision dataset:

```
>>> with h5py.File('big1.hdf5','w') as f1:
...     f1['big'] = bigdata

$ ls -lh big1.hdf5
-rw-r--r-- 1 computer computer 784K Apr 13 14:40 foo.hdf5
```

Or we could request that HDF5 store it as single-precision data:

```
>>> with h5py.File('big2.hdf5','w') as f2:
...     f2.create_dataset('big', data=bigdata, dtype=np.float32)

$ ls -lh big2.hdf5
-rw-r--r-- 1 computer computer 393K Apr 13 14:42 foo.hdf5
```

Keep in mind that whichever one you choose, your data will emerge from the file in that format:

```
>>> f1 = h5py.File("big1.hdf5")
>>> f2 = h5py.File("big2.hdf5")
>>> f1['big'].dtype
dtype('float64')
>>> f2['big'].dtype
dtype('float32')
```

Automatic Type Conversion and Direct Reads

But exactly how and when does the data get converted between the double-precision `float64` in memory and the single-precision `float32` in the file? This question is important for performance; after all, if you have a dataset that takes up 90% of the memory in your computer and you need to make a copy before storing it, there are going to be problems.

The HDF5 library *itself* handles type conversion, and does it on the fly when saving to or reading from a file. Nothing happens at the Python level; your array goes in, and the appropriate bytes come out on disk. There are built-in routines to convert between many source and destination formats, including between all flavors of floating-point and integer numbers available in NumPy.

But what if we want to go the other direction? Suppose we have a single-precision float dataset on disk, and want to read it in as double precision? There are a couple of reasons this might be useful. The result might be very large, and we might not have the memory space to hold both single- and double-precision versions in Python while we do the conversion. Or we might want to do the type conversion on the fly while reading from disk, to reduce the application's runtime.

For big arrays, the best approach is to read directly into a preallocated NumPy array of the desired type. Let's say we have the single-precision dataset from the previous example, and we want to read it in as double precision:

```
>>> dset = f2['big']
>>> dset.dtype
dtype('float32')
>>> dset.shape
(100, 1000)
```

We allocate our new double-precision array on the Python side:

```
>>> big_out = np.empty((100, 1000), dtype=np.float64)
```

Here `np.empty` creates the array, but unlike `np.zeros` or `np.ones` it doesn't bother to initialize the array elements. Now we request that HDF5 read directly into our output array:

```
>>> dset.read_direct(big_out)
```

That's it! HDF5 fills up the empty array with the requested data. No extra arrays or time spent converting.

 When using `read_direct`, you don't always have to read the whole dataset. See "Reading Directly into an Existing Array" on page 34 for details.

Reading with astype

You may not always want to go through the whole rigamarole of creating a destination array and passing it to `read_direct`. Another way to tell HDF5 what type you want is by using the `Dataset.astype` context manager.

Let's suppose we want to read the first 1000 elements of our "big" dataset in the previous example, and have HDF5 itself convert them from single to double precision:

```
>>> with dset.astype('float64'):
...     out = dset[0,:]
>>> out.dtype
dtype('float64')
```

Finally, here are some tips to keep in mind when using HDF5's automatic type conversion. They apply both to reads with `read_direct` or `astype` and also to writing data from NumPy into existing datasets:

1. Generally, you can only convert between types of the same "flavor." For example, you can convert integers to floats, and floats to other floats, but not strings to floats or integers. You'll get an unhelpful-looking `IOError` if you try.

2. When you're converting to a "smaller" type (`float64` to `float32`, or `"S10"` to `"S5"`), HDF5 will truncate or "clip" the values:

```
>>> f.create_dataset('x', data=1e256, dtype=np.float64)
>>> print f['x'][...]
1e+256
>>> f.create_dataset('y', data=1e256, dtype=np.float32)
>>> print f['y'][...]
inf
```

There's no warning when this happens, so it's in your interest to keep track of the types involved.

Reshaping an Existing Array

There's one more trick up our sleeve with `create_dataset`, although this one's a little more esoteric. You'll recall that it takes a "shape" argument as well as a dtype argument. As long as the total number of elements match, you can specify a shape different from the shape of your input array.

Let's suppose we have an array that stores 100 640×480-pixel images, stored as 640-element "scanlines":

```
>>> imagedata.shape
(100, 480, 640)
```

Now suppose that we want to store each image as a "top half" and "bottom half" without needing to do the slicing when we read. When we go to create the dataset, we simply specify the new shape:

```
>>> f.create_dataset('newshape', data=imagedata, shape=(100, 2, 240, 640))
```

There's no performance penalty. Like the built-in `np.reshape`, only the indices are shuffled around.

Fill Values

If you create a brand-new dataset, you'll notice that by default it's zero filled:

```
>>> dset = f.create_dataset('empty', (2,2), dtype=np.int32)
>>> dset[...]
```

```
array([[0, 0],
       [0, 0]])
```

For some applications, it's nice to pick a default value other than 0. You might want to set unmodified elements to -1, or even NaN for floating-point datasets.

HDF5 addresses this with a *fill value*, which is the value returned for the areas of a dataset that haven't been written to. Fill values are handled when data is read, so they don't cost you anything in terms of storage space. They're defined when the dataset is created, and can't be changed:

```
>>> dset = f.create_dataset('filled', (2,2), dtype=np.int32, fillvalue=42)
>>> dset[...]
array([[42, 42],
       [42, 42]])
```

A dataset's fill value is available on the `fillvalue` property:

```
>>> dset.fillvalue
42
```

Reading and Writing Data

Your main day-to-day interaction with `Dataset` objects will look a lot like your interactions with NumPy arrays. One of the design goals for the h5py package was to "recycle" as many NumPy metaphors as possible for datasets, so that you can interact with them in a familiar way.

Even if you're an experienced NumPy user, don't skip this section! There are important performance differences and implementation subtleties between the two that may trip you up.

Before we dive into the nuts and bolts of reading from and writing to datasets, it's important to spend a few minutes discussing how `Dataset` objects *aren't* like NumPy arrays, especially from a performance perspective.

Using Slicing Effectively

In order to use `Dataset` objects efficiently, we have to know a little about what goes on behind the scenes. Let's take the example of reading from an existing dataset. Suppose we have the (100, 1000)-shape array from the previous example:

```
>>> dset = f2['big']
>>> dset
<HDF5 dataset "big": shape (100, 1000), type "<f4">
```

Now we request a slice:

```
>>> out = dset[0:10, 20:70]
>>> out.shape
(10, 50)
```

Here's what happens behind the scenes when we do the slicing operation:

1. h5py figures out the shape (10, 50) of the resulting array object.
2. An empty NumPy array is allocated of shape (10, 50).
3. HDF5 selects the appropriate part of the dataset.
4. HDF5 copies data from the dataset into the empty NumPy array.
5. The newly filled in NumPy array is returned.

You'll notice that this implies a certain amount of overhead. Not only do we create a new NumPy array for each slice requested, but we have to figure out what size the array object should be, check that the selection falls within the bounds of the dataset, and have HDF5 perform the selection, all before we've read a single byte of data.

This leads us to the first and most important performance tip when using datasets: *take reasonably sized slices.*

Here's an example: using our (100, 1000)-shape dataset, which of the following do you think is likely to be faster?

```
# Check for negative values and clip to 0
for ix in xrange(100):
    for iy in xrange(1000):
        val = dset[ix,iy]            # Read one element
        if val < 0: dset[ix, iy] = 0    # Clip to 0 if needed
```

or

```
# Check for negative values and clip to 0
for ix in xrange(100):
    val = dset[ix,:]          # Read one row
    val[ val < 0 ] = 0        # Clip negative values to 0
    dset[ix,:] = val          # Write row back out
```

In the first case, we perform 100,000 slicing operations. In the second, we perform only 100.

This may seem like a trivial example, but the first example creeps into real-world code frequently; using fast in-memory slices on NumPy arrays, it is actually reasonably quick on modern machines. But once you start going through the whole slice-allocate-HDF5-read pipeline outlined here, things start to bog down.

The same applies to writing, although fewer steps are involved. When you perform a write operation, for example:

```
>>> some_dset[0:10, 20:70] = out*2
```

The following steps take place:

1. h5py figures out the size of the selection, and determines whether it is compatible with the size of the array being assigned.
2. HDF5 makes an appropriately sized selection on the dataset.
3. HDF5 reads from the input array and writes to the file.

All of the overhead involved in figuring out the slice sizes and so on, still applies. Writing to a dataset one element at a time, or even a few elements at a time, is a great way to get poor performance.

Start-Stop-Step Indexing

h5py uses a subset of the plain-vanilla slicing available in NumPy. This is the most familiar form, consisting of up to three indices providing a start, stop, and step.

For example, let's create a simple 10-element dataset with increasing values:

```
>>> dset = f.create_dataset('range', data=np.arange(10))
>>> dset[...]
array([0, 1, 2, 3, 4, 5, 6, 7, 8, 9])
```

One index picks a particular element:

```
>>> dset[4]
4
```

Two indices specify a range, ending just before the last index:

```
>>> dset[4:8]
array([4,5,6,7])
```

Three indices provide a "step," or pitch, telling how many elements to skip:

```
>>> dset[4:8:2]
array([4,6])
```

And of course you can get all the points by simply providing :, like this:

```
>>> dset[:]
array([0,1,2,3,4,5,6,7,8,9])
```

Like NumPy, you are allowed to use negative numbers to "count back" from the end of the dataset, with -1 referring to the last element:

```
>>> dset[4:-1]
array([4,5,6,7,8])
```

Unlike NumPy, you can't pull fancy tricks with the indices. For example, the traditional way to reverse an array in NumPy is this:

```
>>> a = np.arange(10)
>>> a
array([0, 1, 2, 3, 4, 5, 6, 7, 8, 9])
>>> a[::-1]
array([9, 8, 7, 6, 5, 4, 3, 2, 1, 0])
```

But if you try it on a dataset, you get the following:

```
>>> dset[::-1]
ValueError: Step must be >= 1 (got -1)
```

Multidimensional and Scalar Slicing

By now you've gotten used to seeing the expression "...," which is used as a slice in examples. This object has the built-in name Ellipsis in the Python world. You can use it as a "stand-in" for axes you don't want to bother specifying:

```
>>> dset = f.create_dataset('4d', shape=(100, 80, 50, 20))
>>> dset[0,...,0].shape
(80, 50)
```

And of course you can get the entire contents by using Ellipsis by itself:

```
>>> dset[...].shape
(100, 80, 50, 20)
```

There is one oddity we should discuss, which is that of *scalar* datasets. In NumPy, there are two flavors of array containing one element. The first has shape (1,), and is an ordinary one-dimensional array. You can get at the value inside by slicing or simple indexing:

```
>>> dset = f.create_dataset('1d', shape=(1,), data=42)
>>> dset.shape
(1,)
>>> dset[0]
42
>>> dset[...]
array([42])
```

Note, by the way, how using Ellipsis provides an array with one element, whereas integer indexing provides the element itself.

The second flavor has shape () (an empty tuple) and can't be accessed by indexing:

```
>>> dset = f.create_dataset('0d', data=42)
>>> dset.shape
()
>>> dset[0]
ValueError: Illegal slicing argument for scalar dataspace
>>> dset[...]
array(42)
```

Note how using Ellipsis has again returned an array, in this case a scalar array.

How can we get the value itself, without it being wrapped in a NumPy array? It turns out there's another way to slice into NumPy arrays (and Dataset objects). You can index with a somewhat bizarre-looking empty tuple:

```
>>> dset[()]
42
```

So keep these in your toolkit:

1. Using Ellipsis gives you all the elements in the dataset (always as an array object).

2. Using an empty tuple "()" gives you all the elements in the dataset, as an array object for 1D and higher datasets, and as a scalar element for 0D datasets.

 To make things even more confusing, you may see code in the wild that uses the .value attribute of a dataset. This is a historical wart that is exactly equivalent to doing dataset[()]. It's long deprecated and not available in modern versions of h5py.

Boolean Indexing

In an earlier example, we used an interesting expression to set negative entries in a NumPy array val to zero:

```
>>> val[ val < 0 ] = 0
```

This is an idiom in NumPy made possible by *Boolean-array indexing*. If val is a NumPy array of integers, then the result of the expression val < 0 is *an array of Booleans*. Its entries are True where the corresponding elements of val are negative, and False elsewhere. In the NumPy world, this is also known as a *mask*.

Crucially, in both the NumPy and HDF5 worlds, you can use a Boolean array as an indexing expression. This does just what you'd expect; it selects the dataset elements where the corresponding index entries are True, and de-selects the rest.

In the spirit of the previous example, let's suppose we have a dataset initialized to a set of random numbers distributed between -1 and 1:

```
>>> data = np.random.random(10)*2 - 1
>>> data
array([ 0.98885498, -0.28554781, -0.17157685, -0.05227003,  0.66211931,
        0.45692186,  0.07123649, -0.40374417,  0.22059144, -0.82367672])
>>> dset = f.create_dataset('random', data=data)
```

Let's clip the negative values to 0, by using a Boolean array:

```
>>> dset[data<0] = 0
>>> dset[...]
```

```
array([ 0.98885498,  0.        ,  0.        ,  0.        ,  0.66211931,
        0.45692186,  0.07123649,  0.        ,  0.22059144,  0.        ])
```

On the HDF5 side, this is handled by transforming the Boolean array into a list of coordinates in the dataset. There are a couple of consequences as a result.

First, for very large indexing expressions with lots of True values, it may be faster to, for example, modify the data on the Python side and write the dataset out again. If you suspect a slowdown it's a good idea to test this.

Second, the expression on the right-hand side has to be either a scalar, or an array with exactly the right number of points. This isn't quite as burdensome a requirement as it might seem. If the number of elements that meet the criteria is small, it's actually a very effective way to "update" the dataset.

For example, what if instead of clipping the negative values to zero, we wanted to flip them and make them positive? We could modify the original array and write the entire thing back out to disk. Or, we could modify just the elements we want:

```
>>> dset[data<0] = -1*data[data<0]
>>> dset[...]
array([ 0.98885498,  0.28554781,  0.17157685,  0.05227003,  0.66211931,
        0.45692186,  0.07123649,  0.40374417,  0.22059144,  0.82367672])
```

Note that the number of elements (five, in this case) is the same on the left- and righthand sides of the preceding assignment.

Coordinate Lists

There's another feature borrowed from NumPy, with a few modifications. When slicing into a dataset, for any axis, instead of a x:y:z-style slicing expression you can supply a list of indices. Let's use our 10-element range dataset again:

```
>>> dset = f['range']
>>> dset[...]
array([0,1,2,3,4,5,6,7,8,9])
```

Suppose we wanted just elements 1, 2, and 7. We could manually extract them one at a time as dset[1], dset[2], and dset[7]. We could also use a Boolean indexing array with its values set to True at locations 1, 2, and 7.

Or, we could simply specify the elements desired using a list:

```
>>> dset[ [1,2,7] ]
array([1,2,7])
```

This may seem trivial, but it's implemented in a way that is much more efficient than Boolean masking for large datasets. Instead of generating a laundry list of coordinates to access, h5py breaks the selection down into contiguous "subselections," which are much faster when multiple axes are involved.

If you're seaching for documentation on the exotic NumPy methods of accessing an array, they are collectively called *fancy indexing*.

Of course, the trade-off is that there are a few differences from the native NumPy coordinate-list slicing approach, which rule out some of the fancier tricks from the NumPy world:

1. Only one axis at a time can be sliced with a list.

2. Repeated elements are not allowed.

3. Indices in the list must be given in increasing order.

Automatic Broadcasting

In a couple of examples so far, we've made slicing assignments in which the number of elements on the left- and right-hand sides were not equal. For example, in the Boolean array example:

```
>>> dset[data<0] = 0
```

This kind of expression is handled by *broadcasting*, similar to the built-in NumPy broadcasting that handles such things where arrays are involved. Used judiciously, it can give your application a performance boost.

Let's consider our (100, 1000)-shape array from earlier; suppose it contained 100 time traces, each 1000 elements long:

```
>>> dset = f2['big']
>>> dset.shape
(100, 1000)
```

Now suppose we want to copy the trace at dset[0,:] and overwrite all the others in the file. We might do this with a for loop:

```
>>> data = dset[0,:]
>>> for idx in xrange(100):
...     dset[idx,:] = data
```

This will work, but it does require us to write the loop, get the boundary conditions right, and of course perform 100 slicing operations.

There's an even easier way, which exploits the built-in efficient broadcasting of h5py:

```
>>> dset[:,:] = dset[0,:]
```

The shape of the array on the righthand side is (1000,); the shape of the selection on the lefthand side is (100, 1000). Since the last dimensions match, h5py repeatedly copies the data across all 100 remaining indices. It's as efficient as you can get; there's only one slicing operation, and the remainder of the time is spent writing data to disk.

Reading Directly into an Existing Array

Finally we come full circle back to `read_direct`, one of the most powerful methods available on the `Dataset` object. It's as close as you can get to the "traditional" C interface of HDF5, without getting into the internal details of h5py.

To recap, you can use `read_direct` to have HDF5 "fill in" data into an existing array, automatically performing type conversion. Last time we saw how to read `float32` data into a `float64` NumPy array:

```
>>> dset.dtype
dtype('float32')
>>> out = np.empty((100, 1000), dtype=np.float64)
>>> dset.read_direct(out)
```

This works, but requires you to read the entire dataset in one go. Let's pick a more useful example. Suppose we wanted to read the first time trace, at `dset[0,:]`, and deposit it into the `out` array at `out[50,:]`. We can use the `source_sel` and `dest_sel` keywords, for *source selection* and *destination selection* respectively:

```
>>> dset.read_direct(out, source_sel=np.s_[0,:], dest_sel=np.s_[50,:])
```

The odd-looking `np.s_` is a gadget that takes slices, in the ordinary array-slicing syntax, and returns a NumPy `slice` object with the corresponding information.

By the way, you don't have to match the shape of your output array to the dataset. Suppose our application wanted to compute the mean of the first 50 data points in each time trace, a common scenario when estimating DC offsets in real-world experimental data. You could do this using the standard slicing techniques:

```
>>> out = dset[:,0:50]
>>> out.shape
(100, 50)
>>> means = out.mean(axis=1)
>>> means.shape
(100,)
```

Using `read_direct` this would look like:

```
>>> out = np.empty((100,50), dtype=np.float32)
>>> dset.read_direct(out, np.s_[:,0:50])   # dest_sel can be omitted
>>> means = out.mean(axis=1)
```

This may seem like a trivial case, but there's an important difference between the two approaches. In the first example, the `out` array is created internally by h5py, used to store the slice, and then thrown away. In the second example, `out` is allocated by the user, and can be reused for future calls to `read_direct`.

There's no real performance difference when using (100, 50)-shape arrays, but what about (10000, 10000)-shape arrays?

Let's check the real-world performance of this. We'll create a test dataset and two functions. To keep things simple and isolate just the performance difference related to the status of out, we'll always read the same selection of the dataset:

```
dset = f.create_dataset('perftest', (10000, 10000), dtype=np.float32)
dset[:] = np.random.random(10000)  # note the use of broadcasting!

def time_simple():
    dset[:,0:500].mean(axis=1)

out = np.empty((10000, 500), dtype=np.float32)
def time_direct():
    dset.read_direct(out, np.s_[:,0:500])
    out.mean(axis=1)
```

Now we'll see what effect preserving the out array has, if we were to put the read in a for loop with 100 iterations:

```
>>> timeit(time_simple, number=100)
14.04414987564087
>>> timeit(time_direct, number=100)
12.045655965805054
```

Not too bad. The difference is 2 seconds, or about a 14% improvement. Of course, as with all optimizations, it's up to you how far you want to go. This "simple" approach is certainly more legible. But when performing multiple reads of data with the same shape, particularly with larger arrays, it's hard to beat read_direct.

 For historical reasons, there also exists a write_direct method. It does the same in reverse; however, in modern versions of h5py it's no more efficient than regular slicing assignment. You're welcome to use it if you want, but there's no performance advantage.

A Note on Data Types

HDF5 is designed to preserve data in any format you want. Occasionally, this means you may get a file whose contents differ from the most convenient format for processing on your system. One example we discussed before is *endianness*, which relates to how multibyte numbers are represented. You can store a 4-byte floating-point number, for example, in memory with the least significant byte first (*little-endian*), or with the most significant byte first (*big-endian*). Modern Intel-style x86 chips use the *little-endian* format, but data can be stored in HDF5 in either fashion.

Because h5py doesn't know whether you intend to process the data you retrieve or ship it off somewhere else, by default data is returned from the file in whatever format it's stored. In the case of "endianness," this is mostly transparent because NumPy supports both flavors. However, there are performance implications. Let's create two NumPy arrays, one little-endian and one big-endian, and see how they perform on an x86 system:

```
>>> a = np.ones((1000,1000), dtype='<f4')  # Little-endian 4-byte float
>>> b = np.ones((1000,1000), dtype='>f4')  # Big-endian 4-byte float
>>> timeit(a.mean, number=1000)
1.684128999710083
>>> timeit(b.mean, number=1000)
3.1886370182037354
```

That's pretty bad, about a factor of 2. If you're processing data you got from somebody else, and your application does lots of long-running calculations, it's worth taking a few minutes to check.

To convert to "native" endianness in this example you basically have three choices: use read_direct with a natively formatted array you create yourself, use the astype context manager, or convert the array manually in place after you read it. For the latter, there's a quick way to convert NumPy arrays in place without making a copy:

```
>>> c = b.view("float32")
>>> c[:] = b
>>> b = c
>>> timeit(b.mean, number=1000)
1.697857141494751
```

This is a general performance issue, not limited to endian considerations. For example, single- versus double-precision floats have performance implications, and even integers can be problematic if you end up using 16-bit integers with code that has values greater than 2^{16}. Keep track of your types, and where possible *use the features HDF5 provides to do conversion for you.*

Resizing Datasets

So far, we've established that datasets have a shape and type, which are set when they're created. The type is fixed and can never be changed. However, the shape *can* be changed, within certain limits.

Let's create a new four-element dataset to investigate:

```
>>> dset = f.create_dataset('fixed', (2,2))
```

Looking at the attributes of dset, we see in addition to the .shape attribute, there's an odd one called maxshape:

```
>>> dset.shape
(2, 2)
>>> dset.maxshape
(2, 2)
```

There's also a `resize` method on the `Dataset` object. Let's see what happens if we try to shrink our dataset from (2,2) to (1,1):

```
>>> dset.resize((1,1))
TypeError: Only chunked datasets can be resized
```

Evidently something is missing. How can we make a dataset resizable?

Creating Resizable Datasets

When you create a dataset, in addition to setting its shape, you have the opportunity to make it resizable up to a certain maximum set of dimensions, called its `maxshape` on the h5py side.

Like `shape`, `maxshape` is specified when the dataset is created, but can't be changed. As you saw earlier, if you don't explicitly choose a `maxshape`, HDF5 will create a non-resizable dataset and set `maxshape = shape`. The dataset will also be created with what's called *contiguous* storage, which prevents the use of `resize`. Chapter 4 has more information on contiguous versus *chunked* storage; for now, it's a detail we can ignore.

Let's try again, this time specifying a `maxshape` for the dataset:

```
>>> dset = f.create_dataset('resizable', (2,2), maxshape=(2,2))
>>> dset.shape
(2, 2)
>>> dset.maxshape
(2, 2)
>>> dset.resize((1,1))
>>> dset.shape
(1, 1)
```

Success! What happens if we change back?

```
>>> dset.resize((2,2))
>>> dset.shape
(2, 2)
>>> dset.resize((2,3))
ValueError: unable to set extend dataset (Dataset: Unable to initialize object)
```

As the name suggests, you can't make the dataset bigger than `maxshape`. But this is annoying. What if you don't know when you create the dataset how big it should be? Should you just provide a very large number in `maxshape` to get around this limitation?

Thankfully, that isn't necessary. HDF5 has the concept of "unlimited" axes to deal with this situation. If an axis is declared as "unlimited," you can make it as big as you want. Simply provide `None` for that axis in the `maxshape` tuple to turn this feature on:

```
>>> dset = f.create_dataset('unlimited', (2,2), maxshape=(2, None))
>>> dset.shape
(2, 2)
>>> dset.maxshape
(2, None)
>>> dset.resize((2,3))
>>> dset.shape
(2, 3)
>>> dset.resize((2, 2**30))
>>> dset.shape
(2, 1073741824)
```

You can mark as many axes as you want as unlimited.

Finally, no matter what you put in maxshape, you can't change the total number of axes. This value, the *rank* of the dataset, is fixed and can never be changed:

```
>>> dset.resize((2,2,2))
TypeError: New shape length (3) must match dataset rank (2)
```

Data Shuffling with resize

NumPy has a set of rules that apply when you change the shape of a dataset. For example, take a simple four-element square array with shape (2, 2):

```
>>> a = np.array([ [1, 2], [3, 4] ])
>>> a.shape
(2, 2)
>>> print a
[[1, 2]
 [3, 4]]
```

If we now resize it to (1, 4), keeping the total number of elements unchanged, the values are still there but rearrange themselves:

```
>>> a.resize((1,4))
>>> print a
[[1, 2, 3, 4]]
```

And finally if we resize it to (1, 10), adding new elements, the new ones are initialized to zero:

```
>>> a.resize((1,10))
>>> print a
[[1 2 3 4 0 0 0 0 0 0]]
```

If you've reshaped NumPy arrays before, you're likely used to this *reshuffling* behavior. HDF5 has a different approach. No reshuffling is ever performed. Let's create a Data set object to experiment on, which has both axes set to unlimited:

```
>>> dset = f.create_dataset('sizetest', (2,2), dtype=np.int32, maxshape=(None,
    None))
>>> dset[...] = [ [1, 2], [3, 4] ]
```

```
>>> dset[...]
array([[1, 2],
       [3, 4]])
```

We'll try the same resizing as in the NumPy example:

```
>>> dset.resize((1,4))
>>> dset[...]
array([[1, 2, 0, 0]])
>>> dset.resize((1,10))
>>> dset[...]
array([[1, 2, 0, 0, 0, 0, 0, 0, 0, 0]])
```

What's going on here? When we changed the shape from (2, 2) to (1, 4), the data at locations `dset[1,0]` and `dset[1,1]` didn't get reshuffled; it was lost. For this reason, you should be very careful when using `resize`; the reshuffling tricks you've learned in the NumPy world will quickly lead to trouble.

Finally, you'll notice that in this case the new elements are initialized to zero. In general, they will be set to the dataset's *fill value* (see "Fill Values" on page 26).

When and How to Use resize

One of the most common questions about HDF5 is how to "append" to a dataset. With `resize`, this can be done if care is taken with respect to performance.

For example, let's say we have another dataset storing 1000-element time traces. However, this time our application doesn't know how many to store. It could be 10, or 100, or 1000. One approach might be this:

```
dset1 = f.create_dataset('timetraces', (1,1000), maxshape=(None, 1000))
def add_trace_1(arr):
    dset1.resize( (dset1.shape[0]+1, 1000) )
    dset1[-1,:] = arr
```

Here, every time a new 1000-element array is added, the dataset is simply expanded by a single entry. But if the number of `resize` calls is equal to the number of insertions, this doesn't scale well, particularly if traces will be added thousands of times.

An alternative approach might be to keep track of the number of insertions and then "trim" the dataset when done:

```
dset2 = f.create_dataset('timetraces2', (5000, 1000), maxshape=(None, 1000))

ntraces = 0
def add_trace_2(arr):
    global ntraces
    dset2[ntraces,:] = arr
    ntraces += 1
```

```
def done():
    dset2.resize((ntraces,1000))
```

In the real world, it takes a little more work than this to get the best performance. We've gone about as far as we can go without discussing how the data is actually stored by HDF5. It's time to talk about storage, and more precisely, *chunks*, in Chapter 4.

How Chunking and Compression Can Help You

So far we have avoided talking about exactly how the data you write is stored on disk. Some of the most interesting features in HDF5, including per-dataset compression, are tied up in the details of how data is arranged on disk.

Before we get down to the nuts and bolts, there's a more fundamental issue we have to discuss: how multidimensional arrays are actually handled in Python and HDF5.

Contiguous Storage

Let's suppose we have a four-element NumPy array of strings:

```
>>> a = np.array([ ["A","B"], ["C","D"] ])
>>> print a
[['A' 'B']
 ['C' 'D']]
```

Mathematically, this is a two-dimensional object. It has two axes, and can be indexed using a pair of numbers in the range 0 to 1:

```
>>> a[1,1]
'D'
```

However, there's no such thing as "two-dimensional" computer memory, at least not in common use. The elements are actually stored in a one-dimensional buffer:

```
'A' 'B' 'C' 'D'
```

This is called *contiguous* storage, because all the elements of the array, whether it's stored on disk or in memory, are stored one after another. NumPy uses a simple set of rules to turn an indexing expression into the appropriate offset into this one-dimensional buffer.

In this case, indexing along the first axis advances us into the buffer in steps (*strides*, in NumPy lingo) of 2, while indexing along the second axis advances us in steps of 1.

For example, the indexing expression a[0,1] is handled as follows:

```
offset = 2*0 + 1*1 -> 1
buffer[offset] -> value "B"
```

 You might notice that there are two possible conventions here: whether the "fastest-varying" index is the last (as previously shown), or the first. This choice is the difference between *row-major* and *column-major* ordering. Python, C, and HDF5 all use *row-major* ordering, as in the example.

By default, all but the smallest HDF5 datasets use contiguous storage. The data in your dataset is flattened to disk using the same rules that NumPy (and C, incidentally) uses.

If you think about it, this means that certain operations are much faster than others. Consider as an example a dataset containing one hundred 640×480 grayscale images. Let's say the shape of the dataset is (100, 480, 640):

```
>>> f = h5py.File("imagetest.hdf5")
>>> dset = f.create_dataset("Images", (100, 480, 640), dtype='uint8')
```

A contiguous dataset would store the image data on disk, one 640-element "scanline" after another. If we want to read the first image, the slicing code would be:

```
>>> image = dset[0, :, :]
>>> image.shape
(480, 640)
```

Figure 4-1(A) shows how this works. Notice that data is stored in "blocks" of 640 bytes that correspond to the last axis in the dataset. When we read in the first image, 480 of these blocks are read from disk, all in one big block.

This leads us to the first rule (really, the only one) for dealing with data on disk, *locality*: reads are generally faster when the data being accessed is all stored together. Keeping data together helps for lots of reasons, not the least of which is taking advantage of caching performed by the operating system and HDF5 itself.

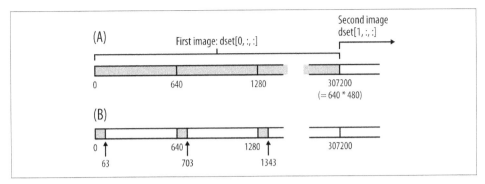

Figure 4-1. Contiguous storage on disk, accessing (A) an entire image all at once, and (B) a 64x64 image tile. Gray regions are the data being retrieved.

It's easy to see that applications reading a whole image, or a series of whole images, will be efficient at reading the data. The advantage of contiguous storage is that the layout on disk corresponds directly to the shape of the dataset: stepping through the last index always means moving through the data in order on disk.

But what if, instead of processing whole images one after another, our application deals with image *tiles*? Let's say we want to read and process the data in a 64×64 pixel slice in the corner of the first image; for example, say we want to add a logo.

Our slicing selection would be:

```
>>> tile = dset[0,0:64,0:64]
>>> tile.shape
(64, 64)
```

Figure 4-1(B) shows how the data is read in this case. Not so good. Instead of reading one nice contiguous block of data, our application has to gather data from all over the place. If we wanted the 64×64 tile from every image at once (dset[:,0:64,0:64]), we'd have to read all the way to the end of the dataset!

The fundamental problem here is that the default contiguous storage mechanism does not match our access pattern.

Chunked Storage

What if there were some way to express this in advance? Isn't there a way to preserve the shape of the dataset, which is semantically important, but tell HDF5 to optimize the dataset for access in 64×64 pixel blocks?

That's what *chunking* does in HDF5. It lets you specify the N-dimensional "shape" that best fits your access pattern. When the time comes to write data to disk, HDF5 splits the data into "chunks" of the specified shape, flattens them, and writes them to disk. The chunks are stored in various places in the file and their coordinates are indexed by a B-tree.

Here's an example. Let's take the (100, 480, 640)-shape dataset just shown and tell HDF5 to store it in chunked format. We do this by providing a new keyword, chunks, to the create_dataset method:

```
>>> dset = f.create_dataset('chunked', (100,480,640), dtype='i1', chunks=
(1,64,64))
```

Like a dataset's type, this quantity, the *chunk shape*, is fixed when the dataset is created and can never be changed. You can check the chunk shape by inspecting the chunks property; if it's None, the dataset isn't using chunked storage:

```
>>> dset.chunks
(1, 64, 64)
```

The chunk shape always has the same number of elements as the dataset shape; in this example, three. Let's repeat the 64×64-pixel slice, as before:

```
>>> dset[0,0:64,0:64]
```

Figure 4-2 shows how this is handled. Much better. In this example, only one chunk is needed; HDF5 tracks it down and reads it from disk in one continuous lump.

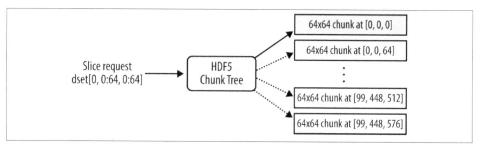

Figure 4-2. HDF5 chunk tree

Even better, since chunked data is stored in nice uniformly sized packets of bytes, you can apply all kinds of operations to it when writing or reading from the file. For example, this is how compression works in HDF5; on their way to and from the disk, chunks are run through a compressor or decompressor. Such *filters* in HDF5 (see "Filters and Compression" on page 48) are completely transparent to the reading application.

Keep in mind that chunking is a storage detail only. You don't need to do anything special to read or write data in a chunked dataset. Just use the normal NumPy-style slicing syntax and let HDF5 deal with the storage.

Setting the Chunk Shape

You are certainly free to pick your own chunk shape, although be sure to read about the performance implications later in this chapter. Most of the time, chunking will be automatically enabled by using features like compression or marking a dataset as resizable. In that case, the *auto-chunker* in h5py will help you pick a chunk size.

Auto-Chunking

If you don't want to sit down and figure out a chunk shape, you can have h5py try to guess one for you by setting chunks to True instead of a tuple:

```
>>> dset = f.create_dataset("Images2", (100,480,640), 'f', chunks=True)
>>> dset.chunks
(13, 60, 80)
```

The "auto-chunker" tries to keep chunks mostly "square" (in N dimensions) and within certain size limits. It's also invoked when you specify the use of compression or other filters without explicitly providing a chunk shape.

By the way, the reason the automatically generated chunks are "square" in N dimensions is that the auto-chunker has no idea what you're planning to do with the dataset, and is hedging its bets. It's ideal for people who just want to compress a dataset and don't want to bother with the details, but less ideal for those with specific time-critical access patterns.

Manually Picking a Shape

Here are some things to keep in mind when working with chunks. The process of picking a chunk shape is a trade-off between the following three constraints:

1. Larger chunks for a given dataset size reduce the size of the chunk B-tree, making it faster to find and load chunks.

2. Since chunks are all or nothing (reading a portion loads the entire chunk), larger chunks also increase the chance that you'll read data into memory you won't use.

3. The HDF5 chunk cache can only hold a finite number of chunks. Chunks bigger than 1 MiB don't even participate in the cache.

So here are the main points to keep in mind:

Do you even need to specify a chunk size?
>   It's best to restrict manual chunk sizing to cases when you know for sure your dataset will be accessed in a way that's likely to be inefficient with either contiguous storage or an auto-guessed chunk shape. And like all optimizations, you should benchmark!

Try to express the "natural" access pattern your dataset will have

As in our example, if you are storing a bunch of images in a dataset and know that your application will be reading particular 64×64 "tiles," you could use N×64×64 chunks (or N×128×128) along the image axes.

Don't make them too small

Keep in mind that HDF5 has to use indexing data to keep track of things; if you use something pathological like a 1-byte chunk size, most of your disk space will be taken up by metadata. A good rule of thumb for most datasets is to keep chunks above 10KiB or so.

Don't make them too big

The key thing to remember is that when you read any data in a chunk, the entire chunk is read. If you only use a subset of the data, the extra time spent reading from disk is wasted. Keep in mind that chunks bigger than 1 MiB by default will not participate in the fast, in-memory "chunk cache" and will instead be read from disk every time.

Performance Example: Resizable Datasets

In the last example of Chapter 3, we discussed some of the performance aspects of resizable datasets. It turns out that with one or two exceptions, HDF5 requires that resizable datasets use chunked storage. This makes sense if you think about how contiguous datasets are stored; expanding any but the last axis would require rewriting the entire dataset!

There are some chunk-related pitfalls when using resizable datasets, one of which illustrates why you have to be careful of using the auto-chunker where performance is critical. It may make decisions that don't match your idea of how the dataset will be used.

Revisiting the example in Chapter 3, let's create two datasets to store a collection of 1000-element-long time traces. The datasets will both be created as expandable along their first axes, and differ only in their initial sizes:

```
>>> dset1 = f.create_dataset('timetraces1', (1, 1000), maxshape=(None, 1000))
>>> dset2 = f.create_dataset('timetraces2', (5000, 1000), maxshape=(None, 1000))
```

Recall that we had two different approaches to "appending" data to these arrays: simple appending (add_trace_1) and overallocate-and-trim (add_trace_2 and done). The second approach was supposed to be faster, as it involved fewer calls to resize:

```
def add_trace_1(arr):
    """ Add one trace to the dataset, expanding it as necessary """
    dset1.resize( (dset1.shape[0]+1, 1000) )
    dset1[-1,:] = arr
```

```
ntraces = 0
def add_trace_2(arr):
    """ Add one trace to the dataset, keeping count of the # of traces
        written """
    global ntraces
    dset2[ntraces,:] = arr
    ntraces += 1

def done():
    """ After all calls to add_trace_2, trim the dataset to size """
    dset2.resize((ntraces,1000))
```

Now, let's actually test the performance with timeit:

```
def setup():
    """ Re-initialize both datasets for the tests """
    global data, N, dset1, dset2, ntraces
    data = np.random.random(1000)
    N = 10000     # Number of iterations
    dset1.resize((1,1000))
    dset2.resize((10001,1000))
    ntraces = 0

def test1():
    """ Add N traces to the first dataset """
    for idx in xrange(N):
        add_trace_1(data)

def test2():
    """ Add N traces to the second dataset, and then trim it """
    for idx in xrange(N):
        add_trace_2(data)
    done()
>>> timeit(test1, setup=setup, number=1)
3.0431830883026123
>>> timeit(test2, setup=setup, number=1)
3.3972668647766113
```

Not quite what we expected. What's going on? One clue comes from inspecting the chunk shape for each dataset:

```
>>> dset1.chunks
(1, 1000)
>>> dset2.chunks
(63, 125)
```

What happened? It turns out that the chunk shape is determined by, among other things, the initial size of the dataset. Let's manually specify a chunk shape and try again. This time we'll set both of them to a shape of (1, 1000), giving us 4k chunks in both cases (1000 elements × 4 bytes):

```
>>> dset1 = f.create_dataset('timetraces3', (1, 1000), maxshape=(None, 1000),
chunks=(1,1000))
```

```
>>> dset2 = f.create_dataset('timetraces4', (5000, 1000), maxshape=(None, 1000),
chunks=(1,1000))
>>> timeit(test1, setup=setup, number=1)
3.0520598888397217
>>> timeit(test2, setup=setup, number=1)
2.5036721229553223
```

Much better. Next, we explore the "killer app" for chunks, arguably even more important than their role in boosting performance: filters.

Filters and Compression

If you wanted to compress a contiguous dataset, you would quickly realize that the entire thing would have to be decompressed and recompressed every time you wrote an element. That's because there's no simple way to index into a compressed dataset using offsets, like you can with an uncompressed contiguous dataset. After all, the point of compression is that you end up with a variable-sized output depending on the values involved.

With chunking, it becomes possible to transparently perform compression on a dataset. The initial size of each chunk is known, and since they're indexed by a B-tree they can be stored anywhere in the file, not just one after another. In other words, each chunk is free to grow or shrink without banging into the others.

The Filter Pipeline

HDF5 has the concept of a *filter pipeline*, which is just a series of operations performed on each chunk when it's written. Each *filter* is free to do anything it wants to the data in the chunk: compress it, checksum it, add metadata, anything. When the file is read, each filter is run in "reverse" mode to reconstruct the original data.

Figure 4-3 shows schematically how this works. You'll notice that since the atomic unit of data here is the *chunk*, reading or writing *any* data (even a single element) will result in decompression of at least one entire chunk. This is one thing to keep in mind when selecting a chunk shape, or choosing whether compression is right for your application.

Finally, you have to specify your filters when the dataset is created, and they can never change.

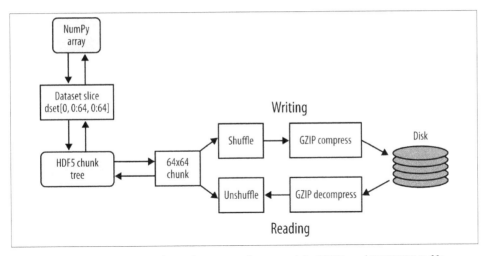

Figure 4-3. HDF5 data pipeline, showing a dataset with GZIP and SHUFFLE filters applied

Compression Filters

A number of compression filters are available in HDF5. By far the most commonly used is the GZIP filter. (You'll also hear this referred to as the "DEFLATE" filter; in the HDF5 world both names are used for the same filter.)

Here's an example of GZIP compression used on a floating-point dataset:

```
>>> dset = f.create_dataset("BigDataset", (1000,1000), dtype='f', compres-
sion="gzip")
>>> dset.compression
'gzip'
```

By the way, you're not limited to floats. The great thing about GZIP compression is that it works with all fixed-width HDF5 types, not just numeric types.

Compression is transparent; data is read and written normally:

```
>>> dset[...] = 42.0
>>> dset[0,0]
42.0
```

Investigating the `Dataset` object, we find a few more properties:

```
>>> dset.compression_opts
4
>>> dset.chunks
(63, 125)
```

The `compression_opts` property (and corresponding keyword to `create_dataset`) reflects any settings for the compression filter. In this case, the default GZIP level is 4.

You'll notice that the auto-chunker has selected a chunk shape for us: (63, 125). Data is broken up into chunks of 63*125*(4 bytes) = 30KiB blocks for the compressor.

The following sections cover some of the available compression filters, and details about each.

 Lots of filters exist for HDF5, and lots more are on the way. If you're archiving data or sharing it with people, it's best to limit yourself to the plain-vanilla GZIP, SHUFFLE, and FLETCHER32 filters, since they are included with HDF5 itself.

GZIP/DEFLATE Compression

As we just saw, GZIP compression is by far the simplest and most portable compressor in HDF5. It ships with every installation of HDF5, and has the following benefits:

- Works with all HDF5 types
- Built into HDF5 and available everywhere
- Moderate to slow speed compression
- Performance can be improved by also using SHUFFLE (see "SHUFFLE Filter" on page 52)

For the GZIP compressor, compression_opts may be an integer from 0 to 9, with a default of 4.

```
>>> dset = f.create_dataset("Dataset", (1000,), compression="gzip")
```

It's also invoked if you specify a number as the argument to compression:

```
>>> dset = f.create_dataset("Dataset2", (1000,), compression=9)
>>> dset.compression
'gzip'
>>> dset.compression_opts
9
```

SZIP Compression

SZIP is a patented compression technology used extensively by NASA. Generally you only have to worry about this if you're exchanging files with people who use satellite data. Because of patent licensing restrictions, many installations of HDF5 have the compressor (but not the decompressor) disabled.

```
>>> dset= myfile.create_dataset("Dataset3", (1000,), compression="szip")
```

SZIP features:

- Integer (1, 2, 4, 8 byte; signed/unsigned) and floating-point (4/8 byte) types only
- Fast compression and decompression
- A decompressor that is almost always available

LZF Compression

For files you'll only be using from Python, LZF is a good choice. It ships with h5py; C source code is available for third-party programs under the BSD license. It's optimized for very, very fast compression at the expense of a lower compression ratio compared to GZIP. The best use case for this is if your dataset has large numbers of redundant data points. There are no `compression_opts` for this filter.

```
>>> dset = myfile.create_dataset("Dataset4", (1000,), compression="lzf")
```

LZF compression:

- Works with all HDF5 types
- Features fast compression and decompression
- Is only available in Python (ships with h5py); C source available

Performance

As always, you should run your own performance tests to see what parts of your application would benefit from attention. However, here are some examples to give you an idea of how the various filters stack up. In this experiment (see h5py.org/lzf for details), a 4 MB dataset of single-precision floats was tested against the LZF, GZIP, and SZIP compressors. A 190 KiB chunk size was used.

First, the data elements were assigned their own indices (see Table 4-1):

```
>>> data[...] = np.arange(1024000)
```

Table 4-1. Compression of trivial data

Compressor	Compression time (ms)	Decompression time (ms)	Compressed by
None	10.7	6.5	0.00%
LZF	18.6	17.8	96.66%
GZIP	58.1	40.5	98.53%
SZIP	63.1	61.3	72.68%

Next, a sine wave with added noise was tested (see Table 4-2):

```
>>> data[...] = np.sin(np.arange(1024000)/32.) + (np.random(1024000)*0.5-0.25)
```

Table 4-2. Compression of noisy data

Compressor	Compression time (ms)	Decompression time (ms)	Compressed by
None	10.8	6.5	0.00%
LZF	65.5	24.4	15.54%
GZIP	298.6	64.8	20.05%
SZIP	115.2	102.5	16.29%

Finally, random float values were used (see Table 4-3):

```
>>> data[...] = np.random(1024000)
```

Table 4-3. Compression of random float data

Compressor	Compression time (ms)	Decompression time (ms)	Compressed by
None	9.0	7.8	0.00%
LZF	67.8	24.9	8.95%
GZIP	305.4	67.2	17.05%
SZIP	120.6	107.7	15.56%

Again, don't take these figures as gospel. Other filters (BLOSC, for example, see "Third-Party Filters" on page 54) are even faster than LZF. It's also rare for an application to spend most of its time compressing or decompressing data, so try not to get carried away with speed testing.

Other Filters

HDF5 includes some extra goodies like consistency check filters and a rearrangement (SHUFFLE) filter to boost compression performance. These filters, and any compression filters you specify, are assembled by HDF5 into the filter pipeline and run one after another.

SHUFFLE Filter

This filter is only ever used in conjunction with a compression filter like GZIP or LZF. It exploits the fact that, for many datasets, most of the entropy occurs in only a few bytes of the type. For example, if you have a 4-byte unsigned integer dataset but your values are generally zero to a few thousand, most of the data resides in the lower two bytes. The first three integers of a dataset might look like this (big-endian format):

```
(0x00 0x00 0x02 0x3E) (0x00 0x00 0x01 0x42) (0x00 0x00 0x01 0x06) ...
```

The SHUFFLE filter repacks the data in the chunk so that all the *first* bytes of the integers are together, then all the *second* bytes, and so on. So you end up with a chunk like this:

```
(0x00 0x00 0x00 ... ) (0x00 0x00 0x00 ... ) (0x02 0x01 0x01 ... ) (0x3E 0x42
0x06 ...)
```

For dictionary-based compressors like GZIP and LZF, it's much more efficient to compress long runs of identical values, like all the zero values collected from the first two bytes of the dataset's integers. There are also savings from the repeated elements at the third byte position. Only the fourth byte position looks really hard to compress.

Here's how to enable the SHUFFLE filter (in conjunction with GZIP):

```
>>> dset = myfile.create_dataset("Data", (1000,), compression="gzip",
shuffle=True)
```

To check if a dataset has SHUFFLE enabled, use the following:

```
>>> dset.shuffle
True
```

The SHUFFLE filter is:

- Available with all HDF5 distributions
- Very, very fast (negligible compared to the compression time)
- Only useful in conjunction with filters like GZIP or LZF

FLETCHER32 Filter

Accidents happen. When you're storing or transmitting a multiterabyte dataset, you'd like to be sure that the bytes that come out of the file are the same ones you put in. HDF5 includes a checksum filter for just this purpose. It uses a 32-bit implementation of Fletcher's checksum, hence the name FLETCHER32.

A checksum is computed when each chunk is written to the file, and recorded in the chunk's metadata. When the chunk is read, the checksum is computed again and compared to the old one. If they don't match, an error is raised and the read fails.

Here's how to enable checksumming for a new dataset:

```
>>> dset = myfile.create_dataset("Data2", (1000,), fletcher32=True)
```

To see if a dataset has checksumming enabled, use the following:

```
>>> dset.fletcher32
True
```

The FLETCHER32 filter is:

- Available with all HDF5 distributions
- Very fast

- Compatible with all lossless filters

Third-Party Filters

Many other filters exist for HDF5. For example, the BLOSC compressor used by the PyTables project (*http://blosc.pytables.org*) is highly tuned for speed. Other filters also exist that are based on the LZO compression system, BZIP2, and more. You can find the most recent list (and contact information for the filter developers) at the HDF Group website (*http://bit.ly/hdf-group-filters*).

There's one more thing to mention, and it's a very new feature (introduced in HDF5 1.8.11): dynamically loaded filters. For the filters listed previously, you have to manually "register" them with the HDF5 library before they can be used. For example, h5py registers the LZF filter when it starts up. Newer versions of HDF5 will automatically load filter modules from disk when they encounter an unknown filter type in a dataset. Dynamic loading is a new technology in HDF5 and support for it in h5py and PyTables is still evolving. Your best bet is to check the h5py and PyTables websites for the most up-to-date information.

And one final reminder: when you use a filter, be *sure* the people you intend to share the data with also have access to it.

## CHAPTER 5

Groups, Links, and Iteration: The "H" in HDF5

So far we've seen how to create `Dataset` objects by giving them a name in the file like `myfile["dataset1"]` or `myfile["dataset2"]`. Unless you're one of those people who stores all their documents on the desktop, you can probably see the flaw in this approach.

Groups are the HDF5 container object, analagous to folders in a filesystem. They can hold datasets and other groups, allowing you to build up a hierarchical structure with objects neatly organized in groups and subgroups.

The Root Group and Subgroups

You may have guessed by now that the `File` object is itself a group. In this case, it also serves as the *root group*, named /, our entry point into the file.

The more general group object is `h5py.Group`, of which `h5py.File` is a subclass. Other groups are easily created by the method `create_group`:

```
>>> f = h5py.File("Groups.hdf5")
>>> subgroup = f.create_group("SubGroup")
>>> subgroup
<HDF5 group "/SubGroup" (0 members)>
>>> subgroup.name
u'/SubGroup'
```

Of course, groups can be nested also. The `create_group` method exists on all `Group` objects, not just `File`:

```
>>> subsubgroup = subgroup.create_group("AnotherGroup")
>>> subsubgroup.name
u'/SubGroup/AnotherGroup'
```

By the way, you don't have to manually create nested groups one at a time. If you supply a full path, HDF5 will create all the intermediate groups for you:

```
>>> out = f.create_group('/some/big/path')
>>> out
<HDF5 group "/some/big/path" (0 members)>
```

The same goes for creating datasets; just supply the full path you want and HDF5 will fill in the missing pieces.

Group Basics

If you remember nothing else from this chapter, remember this: *groups work mostly like dictionaries*. There are a couple of holes in this abstraction, but on the whole it works surprisingly well. Groups are iterable, and have a subset of the normal Python dictionary API.

Let's add another few objects to our file for the examples that follow:

```
>>> f["Dataset1"] = 1.0
>>> f["Dataset2"] = 2.0
>>> f["Dataset3"] = 3.0
>>> subgroup["Dataset4"] = 4.0
```

Dictionary-Style Access

You got a hint of this dictionary-like behavior from the syntax `group[name] = object`. Objects can be retrieved from a group by name:

```
>>> dset1 = f["Dataset1"]
```

Unlike normal Python dictionaries, you can also use POSIX-style paths to directly access objects in subgroups, without having to tediously open all the groups between here and there:

```
>>> dset4 = f["SubGroup/Dataset4"]     # Right
>>> dset4 = f["SubGroup"]["Dataset4"]  # Works, but inefficient
```

Attempting to access an empty group raises `KeyError`, although one irritating thing about h5py is that you don't get the name of the missing object in the exception:

```
>>> f['BadName']
KeyError: "unable to open object (Symbol table: Can't  open object)"
```

There's also the familar `get` method, which is handy if you don't want to raise an exception:

```
>>> out = f.get("BadName")
>>> print out
None
```

You can take the length of a group—note that this measures the number of objects *directly* attached to the group rather than all the objects in nested subgroups:

```
>>> len(f)
5
>>> len(f["SubGroup"])
2
```

Pythonic iteration is also supported using the familiar `iteritems()` and friends (see "Iteration and Containership" on page 65).

Special Properties

There are a few widgets attached to groups (and datasets) that are very useful when working with the hierarchy in a file.

First is the `.file` property. Attached to every object, this gives you a handy way to retrieve a `File` object for the file in which your object resides:

```
>>> f = h5py.File('propdemo.hdf5','w')
>>> grp = f.create_group('hello')
>>> grp.file == f
True
```

This is great when you want to check whether a file is read/write, or just get the filename.

Second is the `.parent` property. This returns the `Group` object that contains your object:

```
>>> grp.parent
<HDF5 group "/" (1 members)>
```

With these two properties, you can avoid most of the path-formatting headaches associated with filesystem work.

Working with Links

What does it mean to give an object a name in the file? From the preceding examples, you might think that the name is part of the object, in the same way that the dtype or shape are part of a dataset.

But this isn't the case. There's a layer between the group object and the objects that are its members. The two are related by the concept of *links*.

Hard Links

Links in HDF5 are handled in much the same way as in modern filesystems. Objects like datasets and groups don't have an intrinsic name; rather, they have an *address* (byte offset) in the file that HDF5 has to look up. When you assign an object to a name in a group, that address is recorded in the group and associated with the name you provided to form a *link*.

Among other things, this means that objects in an HDF5 file can have *more than one name*; in fact, they have as many names as there exist links pointing to them. The number of links that point to an object is recorded, and when no more links exist, the space used for the object is freed.

This kind of a link, the default in HDF5, is called a *hard link* to differentiate it from other kinds of links discussed later in this chapter.

Here's an example of the multiple-name behavior. We'll create a simple file containing a group, and create a hard link to it at /x:

```
>>> f = h5py.File('linksdemo.hdf5','w')
>>> grpx = f.create_group('x')
>>> grpx.name
u'/x'
```

Now we'll create a second link pointing to the group. You can do this using standard Python dictionary-style item assignment:

```
>>> f['y'] = grpx
```

When we retrieve an object from location /y, we get the same group back:

```
>>> grpy = f['y']
>>> grpy == grpx
True
```

You might wonder what happens to the .name property if objects in a file don't have a unique name. Let's see:

```
>>> grpx.name
u'/x'
>>> grpy.name
u'/y'
```

HDF5 makes a best effort to return the name used to retrieve an object. But there's no guarantee. If the object has a name, then you'll generally get one when accessing .name, but it may not be the one you expect.

What does that mean, "if the object has a name"? It's perfectly legal in HDF5 to create an object *without* a name; just supply None:

```
>>> grpz = f.create_group(None)
>>> print grpz.name
None
```

The group grpz in this case exists in the file, but there's no way to get there from the root group. If we were to get rid of the Python object grpz, the group would be deleted and the space in the file reclaimed. To avoid this we can simply link the group into the file structure at our leisure:

```
>>> f['z'] = grpz
>>> grpz.name
u'/z'
```

The multiple names issue also affects the behavior of the .parent property. To address this, in h5py, obj.parent is defined to be the "parent" object according to obj.name. For example, if obj.name is /foo/bar, obj.parent.name will be /foo.

One way to express this is with the posixpath package built into Python:

```
>>> import posixpath
>>> parent = obj.file[posixpath.dirname(obj.name)]
```

To remove links, we use the dictionary-style syntax del group[name]:

```
>>> del f['y']
```

Once all hard links to an object are gone (and the object isn't open somewhere in Python), it's destroyed:

```
>>> del f['x']    # Last hard link; the group is deleted in the file
```

Free Space and Repacking

When an object (for example, a large dataset) is deleted, the space it occupied on disk is reused for new objects like groups and datasets. However, at the time of writing, HDF5 does not track such "free space" across file open/close cycles. So if you don't end up reusing the space by the time you close the file, you may end up with a "hole" of unusable space in the file that can't be reclaimed.

This issue is a high development priority for the HDF Group. In the meantime, if your files seem unusually large you can "repack" them with the h5repack tool, which ships with HDF5:

```
$ h5repack bigfile.hdf5 out.hdf5
```

Soft Links

Those of you who have used Linux or Mac OS X will be familiar with "soft" links. Unlike "hard" links, which associate a link name with a particular object in the file, soft links instead store the *path* to an object.

Here's an example. Let's create a file and populate it with a single group containing a dataset:

```
>>> f = h5py.File('test.hdf5','w')
>>> grp = f.create_group('mygroup')
>>> dset = grp.create_dataset('dataset', (100,))
```

If we were to create a hard link in the root group to the dataset, it would always point to that particular object, even if the dataset were moved or unlinked from mygroup:

```
>>> f['hardlink'] = dset
>>> f['hardlink'] == grp['dataset']
True
>>> grp.move('dataset', 'new_dataset_name')
>>> f['hardlink'] == grp['new_dataset_name']
True
```

Let's move the dataset back, and then create a *soft* link that points to the path /mygroup/dataset. To tell HDF5 that we want to create a soft link, assign an instance of the class h5py.SoftLink to a name in the file:

```
>>> grp.move('new_dataset_name', 'dataset')
>>> f['softlink'] = h5py.SoftLink('/mygroup/dataset')
>>> f['softlink'] == grp['dataset']
True
```

SoftLink objects are very simple; they only have one property, .path, holding the path provided when they are created:

```
>>> softlink = h5py.SoftLink('/some/path')
>>> softlink
<SoftLink to "/some/path">
>>> softlink.path
'/some/path'
```

Keep in mind that instances of h5py.SoftLink are purely a Python-side convenience, not a wrapper around anything in HDF5. Nothing happens until you assign one of them to a name in the file.

Returning to our example, since only the path is stored, if we move the dataset and replace it with something else, /softlink would then point to the new object:

```
>>> grp.move('dataset', 'new_dataset_name')
>>> dset2 = grp.create_dataset('dataset', (50,))
>>> f['softlink'] == dset
False
>>> f['softlink'] == dset2
True
```

Soft links are therefore a great way to refer to "the object which resides at /some/partic ular/path," rather than any specific object in the file. This can be very handy if, for example, a particular dataset represents some information that needs to be updated without breaking all the links to it elsewhere in the file.

The value of a soft link is *not* checked when it's created. If you supply an invalid path (or the object is later moved/deleted), accessing will fail with an exception. Because of how HDF5 reports such an error, you will get the same exception as you would when trying to access a nonexistent name in the group, KeyError:

```
>>> f['broken'] = h5py.SoftLink('/some/nonexistent/object')
>>> f['broken']
KeyError: "unable to open object"
```

By the way, since soft links only record a path, they don't participate in the reference counting that hard links do. So if you have a soft link /softlink pointing at an object hard-linked at /a, if you delete the object (del f["/a"]) it will be destroyed and the soft link will simply break.

 You may be wondering what happens when a broken soft link appears in items() or values(). The answer is that object None is used as the value instead.

External Links

Starting with HDF5 1.8, there's an additional type of link in addition to the file-local hard and soft links. *External links* allow you to refer to objects in other files. They're one of the coolest features of HDF5, but one of the most troublesome to keep track of because of their transparency.

An external link has two components: the name of a file, and then the (absolute) name of an object within that file. Like soft links, you create them with a "marker" object, in this case an instance of h5py.ExternalLink.

Let's create a file with a single object inside, and then link to it from another file:

```
>>> with h5py.File('file_with_resource.hdf5', 'w') as f1:
...     f1.create_group('mygroup')

>>> f2 = h5py.File('linking_file.hdf5', 'w')
>>> f2['linkname'] = h5py.ExternalLink('file_with_resource.hdf5', 'mygroup')
```

Like soft links, external links are transparent, in the sense that if they're not broken, we get back the group or dataset they point to instead of some intermediate object. So if we access the link we just created, we get a group back:

```
>>> grp = f2['linkname']
>>> grp.name
u'/mygroup'
```

However, if we look more closely we discover that this object resides in a different file:

```
>>> grp.file
<HDF5 file "file_with_resource.hdf5" (mode r+)>
>>> f2
<HDF5 file "linking_file.hdf5" (mode r+)>
```

Keep in mind that this can lead to odd-looking consequences. For example, when you use the `.parent` property on the retrieved object, it points to the root group of the external file, not the file in which the link resides:

```
>>> f2['/linkname'].parent == f2['/']
False
```

Both the file and object names are checked when you create the external link. So if HDF5 can't find the file, or the specified object within the file, you'll get an exception:

```
>>> f2['anotherlink'] = h5py.ExternalLink('missing.hdf5','/')
ValueError: unable to create link (Links: Unable to initialize object)
```

The two main hazards when dealing with external links are (1) that the file the link points to won't be around when it's accessed, and (2) by simply traversing the links in the file, you can "wander" into a different file.

There's not too much we can do about (1); it's up to you to keep files organized and be mindful of what links to what. Hazard (2) is a little more dangerous, particularly since all the "Pythonic" methods of accessing group members, like iteration, `items()`, and so on, will include external links. If it's undesirable for your application to cross file boundaries, be sure to check the `.file` property to see where the objects actually reside.

At the moment, there's no way to set a "search path" from h5py. When an external link is encountered, HDF5 will first look for the destination file in the same directory as the file with the link, and then in the current working directory. That's it.

A Note on Object Names

You might have noticed that when you retrieve the name of an object, it comes out as a Python Unicode object:

```
>>> f['/foo'].name
u'/foo'
```

This is intentional, and following the improved Unicode support of HDF5 1.8 (and Python 3) it was introduced in h5py version 2.0. Object names in the file are always treated as "text" strings, which means they represent sequences of characters. In contrast, "byte" strings are sequences of 8-bit numbers that can often but not always store ASCII or Latin-1 encoded text.

The great thing about this is that international characters are supported for all object names in the file; you don't have to "ASCII-ize" anything to fit it into the HDF5 system. Names are stored using the most-compatible storage strategy possible for maximum compatibility with older versions (1.6) of HDF5.

To take advantage of this, simply supply a Unicode string when creating an object or making a new link:

```
>>> grp = f.create_group(u'e_with_accent_\u00E9')
>>> print grp.name
/e_with_accent_é
```

On the backend, h5py converts your string to the HDF5-approved UTF-8 encoding before storing it. When you supply a "regular" or "byte" string (as in most of the previous examples), h5py uses your string as is. It's technically possible to store non-UTF-8 strings like this, although such use is strongly discouraged. If you do happen to receive a file with such "noncompliant" object names, h5py will simply pass back the raw byte string and let you figure it out.

Using get to Determine Object Types

We mentioned that the familiar dictionary-style method get was also available on Group objects, and showed how to handle missing group members without raising KeyError. But this version of get is a little more capable than the Python get.

There are two additional keywords in addition to the dictionary-style default: get class and getlink. The getclass keyword lets you retrieve the *type* of an object without actually having to open it. At the HDF5 level, this only requires reading some metadata and is consequently very fast.

Here's an example: first we'll create a file containing a single group and a single dataset:

```
>>> f = h5py.File('get_demo.hdf5','w')
>>> f.create_group('subgroup')
>>> f.create_dataset('dataset', (100,))
```

Using get, the *type* of object can be retrieved:

```
>>> for name in f:
...     print name, f.get(name, getclass=True)
dataset <class 'h5py._hl.dataset.Dataset'>
subgroup <class 'h5py._hl.group.Group'>
```

The second keyword, getlink, lets you determine the properties of the link involved:

```
>>> f['softlink'] = h5py.SoftLink('/subgroup')
>>> with h5py.File('get_demo_ext.hdf5','w') as f2:
...     f2.create_group('egroup')
>>> f['extlink'] = h5py.ExternalLink('get_demo_ext.hdf5','/egroup')

>>> for name in f:
...     print name, f.get(name, getlink=True)
dataset <h5py._hl.group.HardLink object at 0x047277F0>
extlink <ExternalLink to "/egroup" in file "get_demo_ext.hdf5"
softlink <SoftLink to "/subgroup">
subgroup <h5py._hl.group.HardLink object at 0x047273B0>
```

You'll notice that instances of SoftLink and ExternalLink were returned, complete with path information. This is the official way to retrieve such information after the link is created.

For the hard links at subgroup and dataset, there's also an instance of something called h5py.HardLink. This exists solely to support the use of get; it has no other function and no properties or methods.

Finally, if all you care about is the *kind* of link involved, and not the exact values of the paths and files involved, you can combine the getclass and getlink keywords to return the link class:

```
>>> for name in f:
...     print name, f.get(name, getclass=True, getlink=True)
dataset <class 'h5py._hl.group.HardLink'>
extlink <class 'h5py._hl.group.ExternalLink'>
softlink <class 'h5py._hl.group.SoftLink'>
subgroup <class 'h5py._hl.group.HardLink'>
```

 For many of the classes involved here, you may notice that they were originally defined in the subpackage h5py._hl, for example h5py._hl.group.SoftLink shown earlier. This is an implementation detail that may change; when doing isinstance checks, etc., use the names directly attached to the h5py package (e.g., h5py.SoftLink).

Using require to Simplify Your Application

Unlike Python dictionaries, you can't directly overwrite the members of a group:

```
>>> f = h5py.File('require_demo.hdf5','w')
>>> f.create_group('x')
>>> f.create_group('y')
>>> f.create_group('y')
ValueError: unable to create group (Symbol table: Unable to initialize object)
```

This also holds true for manually hard-linking objects:

```
>>> f['y'] = f['x']
ValueError: unable to create link (Links: Unable to initialize object)
```

This is an intentional feature designed to prevent data loss. Since objects are immediately deleted when you unlink them from a group, you have to explicitly delete the link rather than having HDF5 do it for you:

```
>>> del f['y']
>>> f['y'] = f['x']
```

This leads to some headaches in real-world code. For example, a fragment of analysis code might create a file and write the results to a dataset:

```
>>> data = do_large_calculation()
>>> with h5py.File('output.hdf5') as f:
...     f.create_dataset('results', data=data)
```

If there are many datasets and groups in the file, it might not be appropriate to overwrite the entire file every time the code runs. But if we don't open in w mode, then our program will only work the first time, unless we manually remove the output file every time it runs.

To deal with this, create_group and create_dataset have companion methods called require_group and require_dataset. They do exactly the same thing, only first they check for an existing group or dataset and return it instead.

Both versions take exactly the same arguments and keywords. In the case of require_dataset, h5py also checks the requested shape and dtype against any existing dataset and fails if they don't match:

```
>>> f.create_dataset('dataset', (100,), dtype='i')
>>> f.require_dataset('dataset', (100,), dtype='f')
TypeError: Datatypes cannot be safely cast (existing int32 vs new f)
```

There's a minor detail here, in that a conflict is only deemed to occur if the shapes don't match, or the *requested precision* of the datatype is *higher* than the existing precision. So if there's a preexisting int64 dataset, then require_dataset will succeed if int32 is requested:

```
>>> f.create_dataset('int_dataset', (100,), dtype='int64')
>>> f.require_dataset('int_dataset', (100,), dtype='int32')
```

The NumPy casting rules are used to check for conflicts; you can test the types yourself using np.can_cast.

Iteration and Containership

Iteration is a core Python concept, key to writing "Pythonic" code that runs quickly and that your colleagues can understand. It's also a natural way to explore the contents of groups.

How Groups Are Actually Stored

In the HDF5 file, group members are indexed using a structure called a "B-tree." This isn't a computer science text, so we won't spend too long on the subject, but it's valuable to have a rough understanding of what's going on behind the scenes, especially if you're dealing with groups that have thousands or hundreds of thousands of items.

"B-trees" are data structures that are great for keeping track of large numbers of items, while still making retrieval (and addition) of items fast. They work by taking a collection of items, each of which is orderable according to some scheme like a string name or numeric identifier, and building up a tree-like "index" to rapidly retrieve an item.

For example, if you have an HDF5 group with a single member, and another group with a million members, it *doesn't* take a million times as long to open an object in the latter group. Group members are indexed by name, so if you know the name of an object then HDF5 can traverse the index and quickly retrieve the item. The same is true when creating a new group member; HDF5 doesn't have to "insert" the member into the middle of a big table somewhere, shuffling all the entries around.

Of course, all of this is transparent to the user. Every group in an HDF5 file comes with an index that tracks members in alphabetical order. Keep in mind this means "C-style" alphabetical order (whimsically called "ASCIIbetical" order):

```
>>> f = h5py.File('iterationdemo.hdf5','w')
>>> f.create_group('1')
>>> f.create_group('2')
>>> f.create_group('10')
>>> f.create_dataset('data', (100,))
>>> f.keys()
[u'1', u'10', u'2', u'data']
```

Files can also contain other optional indices, for example those that track object creation time, but h5py doesn't expose them.

This brings us to the first point: h5py will generally iterate over objects in the file in alphabetical order (especially for small groups), but you shouldn't rely on this behavior. Behind the scenes, HDF5 is actually retrieving objects in so-called *native* order, which basically means "as fast as possible." The only thing that's guaranteed is that if you don't modify the group, the order will remain the same.

Dictionary-Style Iteration

In keeping with the general convention that *groups work like dictionaries*, iterating over a group in HDF5 provides the names of the members. Remember, these will be supplied as Unicode strings:

```
>>> [x for x in f]
[u'1', u'10', u'2', u'data']
```

There are also iterkeys (equivalent to the preceding), itervalues, and iteritems methods, which do just what you'd expect:

```
>>> [y for y in f.itervalues()]
[<HDF5 group "/1" (0 members)>,
 <HDF5 group "/10" (0 members)>,
 <HDF5 group "/2" (0 members)>,
 <HDF5 dataset "data": shape (100,), type "<f4">]
```

```
>>> [(x,y) for x, y in f.iteritems()]
[(u'1', <HDF5 group "/1" (0 members)>),
 (u'10', <HDF5 group "/10" (0 members)>),
 (u'2', <HDF5 group "/2" (0 members)>),
 (u'data', <HDF5 dataset "data": shape (100,), type "<f4">)]
```

There are also the standard keys, items, and values methods, which produce lists equivalent to the three preceding examples. This brings us to the first performance tip involving iteration and groups: unless you *really* want to produce a list of the 10,000 objects in your group, use the iter* methods.

 If you're using Python 3, you'll notice that you have only the keys, values, and items methods. That's OK; like dictionaries, under Python 3 these return iterables, not lists.

Containership Testing

This is another seemingly obvious performance issue that crops up from time to time. If you're writing code like this, DON'T:

```
>>> if 'name' in group.keys():
```

This creates and throws away a list of all your group members every time you use it. By instead using the standard Python containership test, you can leverage the underlying HDF5 index on object names, which will go very, very fast:

```
>>> if 'name' in group:
```

Critically, you can also use paths spanning several groups, although it's very slightly slower since the intermediate groups have to be inspected by HDF5:

```
>>> if 'some/big/path' in group:
```

Very handy. Keep in mind that like accessing group members, the POSIX-style "parent directory" symbol ".." *won't work*. You won't even get an error message; HDF5 will look for a group named ".." and determine it's not present:

```
>>> '../1' in f['/1']
False
```

If you're manipulating POSIX-style strings and run into this problem, consider "normalizing" your paths using the posixpath package:

```
>>> grp = f['/1']
>>> path = "../1"

>>> import posixpath as pp
>>> path = pp.normpath(pp.join(grp.name, path))
>>> path
u'/1'
```

```
>>> path in grp
True
```

Multilevel Iteration with the Visitor Pattern

Basic iteration works fine for the contents of a single group. But what if you want to iterate over every single object in the file? Or all objects "below" a certain group?

In the HDF5 world, this is accomplished by *visitor* iteration. Rather than HDF5 supplying you with an iterable, you provide a *callable* and HDF5 calls it with an argument or two for every object.

Visit by Name

Your entry point is the `visit` method on the `Group` class. Let's create a simple file to test it out:

```
>>> f = h5py.File('visit_test.hdf5', 'w')

>>> f.create_dataset('top_dataset', data=1.0)

>>> f.create_group( 'top_group_1' )
>>> f.create_group( 'top_group_1/subgroup_1' )
>>> f.create_dataset('top_group_1/subgroup_1/sub_dataset_1', data=1.0)

>>> f.create_group( 'top_group_2' )
>>> f.create_dataset('top_group_2/sub_dataset_2', data=1.0)
```

We can supply any callable to `visit`, which takes one argument, the object name:

```
>>> def printname(name):
...     print name

>>> f.visit(printname)
top_dataset
top_group_1
top_group_1/subgroup_1
top_group_1/subgroup_1/sub_dataset_1
top_group_2
top_group_2/sub_dataset_2
```

No particular order is guaranteed, except that when `visit` enters a subgroup, all the members will be visited before moving on to the next subgroup. For example, everything under `top_group_1` is listed together, and so is everything under `top_group_2`.

You're not required to visit the entire file; `visit` works just fine on subgroups:

```
>>> grp = f['top_group_1']
>>> grp.visit(printname)
subgroup_1
subgroup_1/sub_dataset_1
```

The *visitor* pattern is a little different from standard Python iteration, but is quite powerful once you get used to it. For example, here's a simple way to get a list of every single object in the file:

```
>>> mylist = []
>>> f.visit(mylist.append)
```

 As with all object names in the file, the names supplied to visit are "text" strings (unicode on Python 2, str on Python 3). Keep this in mind when writing your callbacks.

Multiple Links and visit

Of course, we know that an HDF5 file is not just a simple tree. Hard links are a great way to share objects between groups. But how do they interact with visit?

Let's add a hard link to the subgroup we just explored (top_group_1), and run visit again to see what happens:

```
>>> grp['hardlink'] = f['top_group_2']
>>> grp.visit(printname)
hardlink
hardlink/sub_dataset_2
subgroup_1
subgroup_1/sub_dataset_1
```

Not bad. The group at /top_group_2 is effectively "mounted" in the file at /top_group_1/hardlink, and visit explores it correctly.

Now let's try something a little different. We'll undo that last hard link, and try to trick visit into visiting sub_dataset_1 twice:

```
>>> del grp['hardlink']
>>> grp['hardlink_to_dataset'] = grp['subgroup_1/sub_dataset_1']
>>> grp.visit(printname)
hardlink_to_dataset
subgroup_1
```

What happened? We didn't see sub_dataset_1 in the output this time.

By design, each object in a file will be visited only *once*, regardless of how many links exist to the object. Among other things, this eliminates the possibility of getting stuck in an endless loop, as might happen if some clever person were to try the following:

```
>>> f['/root'] = f['/']
```

There is a trade-off. As we saw in our initial discussion of hard links, there's no such thing as the "original" or "real" name for an object. So if multiple links point to your dataset, when visit supplies a name it may not be the one you expect.

Visiting Items

Given the name supplied to your callback, you could retrieve the object by simply using getitem on the group you're iterating over:

```
>>> def printobj(name):
...     print grp[name]
```

But that's a pain; since the name argument supplied by visit is a *relative* path, your function has to know in advance what group it'll be applied to. The previous example will work properly only when applied to grp.

Thankfully, HDF5 provides a more general way to deal with this. The method visit items supplies both the relative name and an instance of each object:

```
>>> def printobj2(name, obj):
...     print name, obj

>>> grp.visititems(printobj2)
hardlink_to_dataset <HDF5 dataset "hardlink_to_dataset": shape (), type "<f8">
subgroup_1 <HDF5 group "/top_group_1/subgroup_1" (1 members)>
```

Since each object has to be opened, there is some overhead involved. You're better off using visititems only in the case where you really need access to each object; for example, if you need to inspect attributes.

One way to make visit a little more generic is by using the built-in Python widget functools.partial. For example, here's a trivial function that prints the absolute path of each object in the group:

```
>>> import posixpath
>>> from functools import partial

>>> def print_abspath(somegroup, name):
...     """ Print *name* as an absolute path
...         somegroup: HDF5 base group (*name* is relative to this)
...         name:      Object name relative to *somegroup*
...     """
...     print posixpath.join(somegroup.name, name)

>>> grp.visit(partial(print_abspath, grp))
/top_group_1/hardlink_to_dataset
/top_group_1/subgroup_1
```

Using this technique, you can avoid "embedding" the group you intend to iterate over in the function itself.

Canceling Iteration: A Simple Search Mechanism

There's a simple way to "bail out" when visiting items. You might notice that our print name function has no explicit return value; in Python that means that the function returns None. If you return anything else, the `visit` or `visititems` method will immediately stop *and return that value*.

Let's suppose that we want to find a dataset that has an attribute with a particular value:

```
>>> f['top_group_2/sub_dataset_2'].attrs['special'] = 42
```

Here's a function that will find such an object, when supplied to `visititems`:

```
>>> def findspecial(name, obj):
...     if obj.attrs.get('special') == 42:
...         return obj

>>> out = f.visititems(findspecial)
>>> out
<HDF5 dataset "sub_dataset_2": shape (), type "<f8">
```

Copying Objects

HDF5 includes built-in facilities for copying objects from one place to another, freeing you from the tedious job of recursively walking the HDF5 tree, checking for duplicate links, copying over attributes, etc.

Single-File Copying

Let's create a simple file to test this, with two groups and a dataset:

```
>>> f = h5py.File('copytest','w')
>>> f.create_group('mygroup')
>>> f.create_group('mygroup/subgroup')
>>> f.create_dataset('mygroup/apples', (100,))
```

Copying a dataset is straightforward, and results in a brand-new dataset, not a reference or link to the old one:

```
>>> f.copy('/mygroup/apples', '/oranges')
>>> f['oranges'] == f['mygroup/apples']
False
```

The great thing about the built-in HDF5 `copy()` is that it correctly handles recursively copying groups:

```
>>> f.copy('mygroup', 'mygroup2')
>>> f.visit(printname)
oranges
mygroup
mygroup/apples
mygroup/subgroup
mygroup2
mygroup2/apples
mygroup2/subgroup
```

You're not limited to using paths for source and destination. If you already have an open Dataset object, for example, you can copy it to a Group or File object:

```
>>> dset = f['/mygroup/apples']
>>> f.copy(dset, f)
>>> f.visit(printname)
apples
oranges
mygroup
mygroup/dataset
mygroup/subgroup
mygroup2
mygroup2/dataset
mygroup2/subgroup
```

Since the destination is a group, the dataset is created with its "base name" of apples, analagous to how files are moved with the UNIX cp command.

There's no requirement that the source and destination be the same file. This is one of the advantages of using File or Group objects instead of paths; the corresponding objects will be copied regardless of which file they reside in. If you're trying to write generic code, it's good to keep this in mind.

Object Comparison and Hashing

Let's take a break from links and iteration to discuss a more subtle aspect of how HDF5 behaves. In lots of the preceding examples, we used Python's equality operator to see if two groups are "the same thing":

```
>>> f = h5py.File('objectdemo.hdf5','w')
>>> grpx = f.create_group('x')
>>> grpy = f.create_group('y')
>>> grpx == f['x']
True
>>> grpx == grpy
False
```

If we investigate further, we discover that this kind of equality testing is independent of whether the Python objects are one and the same:

```
>>> id(grpx)  # Uniquely identifies the Python object "grpx"
73399280
>>> id(f['x'])
73966416
```

In h5py, equality testing uses the low-level HDF5 facilities to determine which references (*identifiers*, in the HDF5 lingo) point to the same groups or datasets on disk. This information is also used to compute the hash of an object, which means you can safely use Group, File, and Dataset objects as dictionary keys or as the members of sets:

```
>>> hash(grpx)
587327447
>>> hash(f['x'])
587327447
```

There's one more wrinkle for equality testing, and you may bump into it when using the .file property on objects: File and Group instances will compare equally when the Group instance represents the root group:

```
>>> f == f['/']
True
```

This is a consequence of the "double duty" File instances perform, representing both your file on disk and also the root group on the HDF5 side.

Finally, the truth value of an HDF5 object lets you see whether it's alive or dead:

```
>>> bool(grpx)
True
>>> f.close()
>>> grpx
<Closed HDF5 group>
>>> bool(grpx)
False
```

Next, we discuss one thing that makes HDF5 so useful in real-world science: the ability to store data and metadata together side by side using attributes.

## CHAPTER 6

Storing Metadata with Attributes

Groups and datasets are great for keeping data organized in a file. But the feature that really turns HDF5 into a scientific database, instead of just a file format, is *attributes*.

Attributes are pieces of metadata you can stick on objects in the file. They can hold equipment settings, timestamps, computation results, version numbers, virtually anything you want. They're a key mechanism for making *self-describing* files. Unlike simple binary formats that just hold arrays of numbers, judicious use of metadata makes your files scientifically useful all on their own.

Attribute Basics

You can attach attributes to any kind of object that is linked into the HDF5 tree structure: groups, datasets, and even named datatypes. To demonstrate, let's create a new file containing a single dataset:

```
>>> f = h5py.File('attrsdemo.hdf5','w')
>>> dset = f.create_dataset('dataset',(100,))
```

Looking at the properties attached to the dset object, there's one called .attrs:

```
>>> dset.attrs
<Attributes of HDF5 object at 73767504>
```

This is a little proxy object (an instance of h5py.AttributeManager) that lets you interact with attributes in a Pythonic way. As was the case with groups, the main thing to keep in mind here is that the attrs object works mostly like a Python dictionary.

For example, you can create a new attribute simply by assigning a name to a value:

```
>>> dset.attrs['title'] = "Dataset from third round of experiments"
>>> dset.attrs['sample_rate'] = 100e6    # 100 MHz digitizer setting
>>> dset.attrs['run_id'] = 144
```

When retrieving elements, we get back the actual value, not an intermediate object like a Dataset:

```
>>> dset.attrs['title']
'Dataset from third round of experiments'
>>> dset.attrs['sample_rate']
100000000.0
>>> dset.attrs['run_id']
144
```

Like groups (and Python dictionaries), iterating over the .attrs object provides the attribute names:

```
>>> [x for x in dset.attrs]
[u'title', u'sample_rate', u'run_id']
```

You'll notice that like object names, the names of attributes are always returned as "text" strings; this means unicode on Python 2, which explains the u prefix.

Attributes don't have the same strict rules as groups for item deletion. You can freely overwrite attributes just by reusing the name:

```
>>> dset.attrs['another_id'] = 42
>>> dset.attrs['another_id'] = 100
```

Trying to access missing attributes raises KeyError, although as with Group you don't get the name of the missing attribute:

```
>>> del dset.attrs['another_id']
>>> dset.attrs['another_id']
KeyError: "can't open attribute (Attribute: Can't open object)"
```

There are also the usual methods like iterkeys, iteritems, values, and so on. They all do what you expect:

```
>>> [(name, val) for name, val in dset.attrs.iteritems()]
[(u'title', 'Dataset from third round of experiments'),
 (u'sample_rate', 100000000.0),
 (u'run_id', 144)]
```

There generally aren't that many attributes attached to an object, so worrying about items versus iteritems, etc., is less important from a performance perspective.

There is also a get method that (unlike the Group version) is a dictionary-style get:

```
>>> dset.attrs.get('run_id')
144
>>> print dset.attrs.get('missing')
None
```

Type Guessing

When you create a dataset, you generally specify the data type you want by providing a NumPy dtype object. There are exceptions; for example, you can get a single-precision float by omitting the dtype when calling `create_dataset`. But every dataset has an explicit dtype, and you can always discover what it is via the `.dtype` property:

```
>>> dset.dtype
dtype('float32')
```

In contrast, with attributes h5py generally hides the type from you. It's important to remember that there *is* a definite type in the HDF5 file. The dictionary-style interface to attributes just means that it's usually inferred from what you provide.

Let's flush our file to disk with:

```
>>> f.flush()
```

and look at it with `h5ls`:

```
$ h5ls -vlr attrsdemo.hdf5
Opened "attrsdemo.hdf5" with sec2 driver.
/                       Group
    Location:  1:96
    Links:     1
/dataset                Dataset {100/100}
    Attribute: run_id    scalar
        Type:       native int
        Data:  144
    Attribute: sample_rate scalar
        Type:       native double
        Data:  1e+08
    Attribute: title     scalar
        Type:       variable-length null-terminated ASCII string
        Data:  "Dataset from third round of experiments"
    Location:  1:800
    Links:     1
    Storage:   400 logical bytes, 0 allocated bytes
    Type:      native float
```

In most cases, the type is determined by simply passing the value to `np.array` and then storing the resulting object. For integers on 32-bit systems you would get a 32-bit ("native") integer:

```
>>> np.array(144).dtype
dtype('int32')
```

This explains the "native int" type for `run_id`.

You're not limited to scalar values, by the way. There's no problem storing whole NumPy arrays in the file:

```
>>> dset.attrs['ones'] = np.ones((100,))
>>> dset.attrs['ones']
array([ 1.,   1.,   1.,   1.,   1.,   1.,   1.,   1.,   1.,   1.,   1.,   1.,   1.,
        1.,   1.,   1.,   1.,   1.,   1.,   1.,   1.,   1.,   1.,   1.,   1.,   1.,
        1.,   1.,   1.,   1.,   1.,   1.,   1.,   1.,   1.,   1.,   1.,   1.,   1.,
        1.,   1.,   1.,   1.,   1.,   1.,   1.,   1.,   1.,   1.,   1.,   1.,   1.,
        1.,   1.,   1.,   1.,   1.,   1.,   1.,   1.,   1.,   1.,   1.,   1.,   1.,
        1.,   1.,   1.,   1.,   1.,   1.,   1.,   1.,   1.,   1.,   1.,   1.,   1.,
        1.,   1.,   1.,   1.,   1.,   1.,   1.,   1.,   1.,   1.,   1.,   1.,   1.,
        1.,   1.,   1.,   1.,   1.,   1.,   1.,   1.,   1.])
```

There are limits, though. In HDF5, with the default settings ("compact" storage, as opposed to "dense" storage), attributes are limited to a size of 64k. For example, if we try to store a (100, 100) array, it complains:

```
>>> dset.attrs['ones'] = np.ones((100, 100))
ValueError: unable to create attribute (Attribute: Unable to initialize object)
```

Most regrettably, we discover that in this case the previous attribute was wiped out:

```
>>> dset.attrs['ones']
KeyError: "can't open attribute (Attribute: Can't open object)"
```

 This is one of the (very few) cases where h5py's interaction with the file is not atomic. Exercise caution with larger array attributes.

One way around this limitation is simply to store the data in a dataset, and link to it with an object reference (see Chapter 8):

```
>>> ones_dset = f.create_dataset('ones_data', data=np.ones((100,100)))
>>> dset.attrs['ones'] = ones_dset.ref
>>> dset.attrs['ones']
<HDF5 object reference>
```

To access the data, use the reference to retrieve the dataset and read it out:

```
>>> ones_dset = f[dset.attrs['ones']]
>>> ones_dset[...]
array([[ 1.,   1.,   1., ...,   1.,   1.,   1.],
       [ 1.,   1.,   1., ...,   1.,   1.,   1.],
       [ 1.,   1.,   1., ...,   1.,   1.,   1.],
       ...,
       [ 1.,   1.,   1., ...,   1.,   1.,   1.],
       [ 1.,   1.,   1., ...,   1.,   1.,   1.],
       [ 1.,   1.,   1., ...,   1.,   1.,   1.]])
```

Strings and File Compatibility

There are a couple of types that have special handling. First, there is a subtle difference in HDF5 regarding the type of a string. In the previous example, we assigned a Python string as an attribute. That created a *variable-length* ASCII string ("Variable-Length Strings" on page 89).

In contrast, an instance of `np.string_` would get stored as a *fixed-length* string in the file:

```
>>> dset.attrs['title_fixed'] = np.string_("Another title")
```

This generally isn't an issue, but some older FORTRAN-based programs can't deal with variable-length strings. If this is a problem for your application, use `np.string_`, or equivalently, arrays of NumPy type S.

By the way, you can also store Unicode strings in the file. They're written out with the HDF5-approved UTF-8 encoding:

```
>>> dset.attrs['Yet another title'] = u'String with accent (\u00E9)'
>>> f.flush()
```

Here's what the file looks like now, with our fixed-length and Unicode strings inside:

```
$ h5ls -vlr attrsdemo.hdf5/dataset
Opened "attrsdemo.hdf5" with sec2 driver.
dataset                  Dataset {100/100}
    Attribute: Yet\ another\ title scalar
        Type:       variable-length null-terminated UTF-8 string
        Data:       "String with accent (\37777777703\37777777651)"
    Attribute: ones       scalar
        Type:       object reference
        Data:       DATASET-1:70568
    Attribute: run_id      scalar
        Type:       native int
        Data:       144
    Attribute: sample_rate scalar
        Type:       native double
        Data:       1e+08
    Attribute: title      scalar
        Type:       variable-length null-terminated ASCII string
        Data:       "Dataset from third round of experiments"
    Attribute: title_fixed scalar
        Type:       13-byte null-padded ASCII string
        Data:       "Another title"
    Location:   1:800
    Links:      1
    Storage:    400 logical bytes, 0 allocated bytes
    Type:       native float
```

There is one more thing to mention about strings, and it has to do with the strict separation in Python 3 between *byte* strings and *text* strings.

When you read an attribute from a file, you generally get an object with the same type as in HDF5. So if we were to store a NumPy int32, we would get an int32 back.

In Python 3, this means that most of the HDF5 strings "in the wild" would be read as *byte* strings, which are very awkward to deal with. So in Python 3, scalar strings are always converted to text strings (type `str`) when they are read.

Python Objects

The question of storing generic Python objects in HDF5 comes up now and then. You'll notice that you can't store an arbitrary object as an attribute (or indeed, as a dataset) in HDF5:

```
>>> dset.attrs['object'] = {}
TypeError: Object dtype dtype('object') has no native HDF5 equivalent
```

This is intentional. As the error message suggests, HDF5 has no "native," built-in type to represent a Python object, and serialized objects in a portability-oriented format like HDF5 are generally recognized as bad news. Storing data in "blob" form defeats the wonderful type system and interoperability of HDF5.

However, I can't tell you how to write your application. If you really want to store Python objects, the best way to do so is by "pickling" (serializing) them to a string:

```
>>> import pickle
>>> pickled_object = pickle.dumps({'key': 42}, protocol=0)
>>> pickled_object
"(dp0\nS'key'\np1\nI42\ns."
>>> dset.attrs['object'] = pickled_object
>>> obj = pickle.loads(dset.attrs['object'])
>>> obj
{'key': 42}
```

You will have to manually keep track of which strings are pickled objects. Technically strings created in this fashion support only ASCII characters, so it's best to stick with pickle protocol "0."

Explicit Typing

Sometimes, for external compatibility, you may need to create attributes with very precise data types and the default type guessing won't do. Or, you may have received a file from a colleague and don't want to change the types of attributes by overwriting them.

There are a couple of mechanisms to deal with this. The `.attrs` proxy object has a method `create`, which takes a name, value, *and* a dtype:

```
>>> f = h5py.File('attrs_create.hdf5','w')
>>> dset = f.create_dataset('dataset', (100,))
>>> dset.attrs.create('two_byte_int', 190, dtype='i2')
>>> dset.attrs['two_byte_int']
190
>>> f.flush()
```

Looking at the file in h5ls:

```
$ h5ls -vlr attrs_create.hdf5
Opened "attrs_create.hdf5" with sec2 driver.
/                              Group
    Location:  1:96
    Links:     1
/dataset                       Dataset {100/100}
    Attribute: two_byte_int scalar
        Type:       native short
        Data:   190
    Location:  1:800
    Links:     1
    Storage:   400 logical bytes, 0 allocated bytes
    Type:       native float
```

This is a great way to make sure you get the right *flavor* of string. Unlike scalar strings, by default when you provide an array-like object of strings, they get sent through NumPy and end up as fixed-length strings in the file:

```
>>> dset.attrs['strings'] = ["Hello", "Another string"]
>>> dset.attrs['strings']
array(['Hello', 'Another string'],
      dtype='|S14')
```

In contrast, if you specify the "variable-length string" special dtype (see Chapter 7):

```
>>> dt = h5py.special_dtype(vlen=str)
>>> dset.attrs.create('more_strings', ["Hello", "Another string"], dtype=dt)
>>> dset.attrs['more_strings']
array([Hello, Another string], dtype=object)
```

Looking at the file, the two attributes have subtly different storage techniques. The original attribute is stored as a pair of 14-byte fixed-length strings, while the other is stored as a pair of variable-length strings:

```
$ h5ls -vlr attrs_create.hdf5
Opened "attrs_create.hdf5" with sec2 driver.
/                              Group
    Location:  1:96
    Links:     1
/dataset                       Dataset {100/100}
    Attribute: more_strings {2}
        Type:       variable-length null-terminated ASCII string
        Data:   "Hello", "Another string"
    Attribute: strings   {2}
        Type:       14-byte null-padded ASCII string
        Data:   "Hello" '\000' repeats 8 times, "Another string"
    Attribute: two_byte_int scalar
        Type:       native short
        Data:   190
    Location:  1:800
    Links:     1
```

```
Storage:    400 logical bytes, 0 allocated bytes
Type:       native float
```

It may seem like a small distinction, but when talking to third-party code this can be the difference between a working program and an error message.

Finally, there's another convenience method called modify, which as the name suggests preserves the type of the attribute:

```
>>> dset.attrs.modify('two_byte_int', 33)
>>> dset.attrs['two_byte_int']
33
```

Keep in mind this may have unexpected consequences when the type of the attribute can't hold the value you provide. In this case, the value will clip:

```
>>> dset.attrs.modify('two_byte_int', 40000)
>>> dset.attrs['two_byte_int']
32767
```

Real-World Example: Accelerator Particle Database

Here's an example of how the groups, datasets, and attributes in HDF5 can be combined to solve a real-world data management problem. Recently, the University of Colorado installed a new electrostatic dust accelerator facility under a grant from NASA. This device fires charged micrometer-sized dust grains into a target chamber at speeds ranging from 1–100 km/s, to simulate the impact of dust grains on surfaces and hardware in space.

Application Format on Top of HDF5

The machine generates huge quantities of data. Every particle, and there can be up to 10 per second for hours on end, generates three digitized waveforms 100,000 points long. A computer system analyzes these waveforms to figure out what the mass of the particle is and how fast it's going. The resulting waveforms and speed/mass estimates are recorded in an HDF5 file for use by the project scientists.

So the basic unit is a particle "event," which has three floating-point waveforms, each of which has some other properties like sampling rate, digitizer range, etc. Then for each event we have metadata estimating particle mass and speed, as well as some top-level metadata like a file timestamp.

Let's use h5ls to peek inside one of these files:

```
Opened "November_Run3.hdf5" with sec2 driver.
/                        Group
    Attribute: timestamp scalar
        Type:      native long long
        Data:  1352843341201
```

```
    Attribute: version_number scalar
        Type:       native int
        Data:   1
    Location:   1:96
    Links:      1
/0                      Group
    Attribute: experiment_name scalar
        Type:       5-byte null-terminated ASCII string
        Data:   "Run3"
    Attribute: id_dust_event scalar
        Type:       native long long
        Data:   210790
    Attribute: mass      scalar
        Type:       native float
        Data:   3.81768e-17
    Attribute: velocity  scalar
        Type:       native float
        Data:   9646.3
    Location:   1:11637136
    Links:      1

/0/first_detector       Dataset {100000/100000}
    Attribute: dt       scalar
        Type:       native float
        Data:   2e-08
    Location:   1:16048056
    Links:      1
    Storage:    400000 logical bytes, 400000 allocated bytes, 100.00% utilization
    Type:       native float

/0/second_detector      Dataset {100000/100000}
    Attribute: dt       scalar
        Type:       native float
        Data:   2e-08
    Location:   1:16449216
    Links:      1
    Storage:    400000 logical bytes, 400000 allocated bytes, 100.00% utilization
    Type:       native float

/0/third_detector       Dataset {100000/100000}
    Attribute: dt       scalar
        Type:       native float
        Data:   2e-08
    Location:   1:16449616
    Links:      1
    Storage:    400000 logical bytes, 400000 allocated bytes, 100.00% utilization
    Type:       native float

/1                      Group
...
```

There's a lot going on here, but it's pretty straightforward. The root group has attributes for a timestamp (when the file was written), along with a version number for the "format" used to structure the file using groups, datasets, and attributes.

Then each particle that goes down the beamline has its own group. The group attributes record the analyzed mass and velocity, along with an integer that uniquely identifies the event. Finally, the three waveforms with our original data are recorded in the particle group. They also have an attribute, in this case giving the sampling interval of the time series.

Analyzing the Data

The crucial thing here is that the *metadata* required to make sense of the raw waveforms is stored *right next to the data*. For example, time series like our waveforms are useless unless you also know the time spacing of the samples. In the preceding file, that time interval (dt) is stored as an attribute on the waveform dataset. If we wanted to plot a waveform with the correct time scaling, all we have to do is:

```
import pyplot as p
f = h5py.File("November_Run3.hdf5",'r')

# Retrieve HDF5 dataset
first_detector = f['/0/first_detector']

# Make a properly scaled time axis
x_axis = np.arange(len(first_detector))*first_detector.attrs['dt']

# Plot the result
p.plot(x_axis, first_detector[...])
```

There's another great way HDF5 can simplify your analysis. With other formats, it's common to have an input file or files, a code that processes them, and a "results" file with the output of your computation. With HDF5, you can have *one* file containing both the input data and the results of your analysis.

For example, suppose we wrote a piece of code that determined the electrical charge on the particle from the waveform data. We can store this right in the file next to the estimates for mass and velocity:

```
from some_science_package import charge_estimator

def update_particle_group(grp):

    # Retrieve waveform data
    first_det = grp['first_detector'][...]
    second_det = grp['second_detector'][...]

    # Retrieve time scaling data
    dt = grp['first_detector'].attrs['dt']
```

```
        # Perform charge estimation
        charge = charge_estimator(first_det, second_det, interval=dt)

        # Write charge to file
        grp.attrs['charge'] = charge
        print "For group %s, got charge %.2g" % (grp.name, charge)
>>> for grp in f.itervalues():
...     update_particle_group(grp)
```

The same goes for analysis that creates output datasets instead of just scalars. The key
point here is to transition from thinking of the HDF5 container as a *file* to treating it as
a *database*.

 Don't get carried away. Keep backups of your data in case you accidentally do something wrong.

We've covered the four main objects in the HDF5 universe: files, groups, datasets, and
attributes. Now it's time to take a break and talk about the HDF5 *type* system, and what
it can do for you.

## CHAPTER 7

More About Types

One of the best features of HDF5 is the huge variety of datatypes it supports. In some cases, the HDF5 feature set goes beyond NumPy. To maintain performance and create interoperable files, it's important to understand exactly what's going on when you use each type.

The HDF5 Type System

As with NumPy, all data in HDF5 has an associated type. The HDF5 type system is quite flexible and includes the usual suspects like integers and floats of various precisions, as well as strings and vector types.

Table 7-1 shows the native HDF5 datatypes and how they map to NumPy. Keep in mind that most of the types (integers and floats, for example) support a number of different precisions. For example, on most NumPy installations integers come in 1-, 2-, 4-, and 8-byte widths.

Table 7-1. HDF5 types

Native HDF5 type	NumPy equivalent
Integer	`dtype("i")`
Float	`dtype("f")`
Strings (fixed width)	`dtype("S10")`
Strings (variable width)	`h5py.special_dtype(vlen=bytes)`
Compound	`dtype([ ("field1": "i"), ("field2": "f") ])`
Enum	`h5py.special_dtype(enum=("i",{"RED":0, "GREEN":1, "BLUE":2}))`
Array	`dtype("(2,2)f")`
Opaque	`dtype("V10")`
Reference	`h5py.special_dtype(ref=h5py.Reference)`

The h5py package (and PyTables) implement a few additional types on top of this system. Table 7-2 lists additions made by h5py that are described in this chapter.

Table 7-2. Additional Python-side types

Python type	NumPy expression	Stored as
Boolean	np.dtype("bool")	HDF5 enum with FALSE=0, TRUE=1
Complex	np.dtype("complex")	HDF5 compound with fields *r* and *i*

Integers and Floats

HDF5 supports all the NumPy integer sizes (1 byte to 8 bytes), signed and unsigned, little-endian and big-endian. Keep in mind that the default behavior for HDF5 when storing a too-large value in a too-small dataset is to *clip*, not to "roll over" like some versions of NumPy:

```
>>> f = h5py.File("typesdemo.hdf5")
>>> dset = f.create_dataset('smallint', (10,), dtype=np.int8)
>>> dset[0] = 300
>>> dset[0]
127
>>> a = np.zeros((10,), dtype=np.int8)
>>> a[0] = 300
>>> a[0]
-44
```

For floating-point numbers, HDF5 supports both single- and double-precision floats (4 and 8 bytes respectively) out of the box.

The HDF5 type representation system is very powerful, and among other things it can represent unusual floating-point precisions. "Half-precision" floats are an interesting case. These tiny 2-byte floats, available in NumPy as `float16`, are used for storage in applications like image and video processing, since they consume only half the space of the equivalent single-precision float. They're great where precision isn't that important and more dynamic range is needed than a 16-bit integer can provide.

```
>>> dset = f.create_dataset('half_float', (100,100,100), dtype=np.float16)
```

Keep in mind this is a storage format only; trying to do math on half-precision floats in NumPy will require casting and therefore be slow. Use `Dataset.read_direct`, the `Dataset.astype` context manager, or simply convert them after reading:

```
>>> a = dset[...]
>>> a = a.astype(np.float32)
```

But if you have values roughly between 10^{-8} and 60,000, and aren't too bothered about precision, they're a great way to save disk space.

Fixed-Length Strings

Strings in HDF5 are a bit of a pain; you got a taste of that in Chapter 6.

As we'll see in the next section, most real-world strings don't fit neatly into a constant amount of storage. But fixed-width strings have been around since the FORTRAN days and fit nicely into the NumPy world.

In NumPy, these are generally created using the "S" dtype. This is a *flexible* dtype that lets you set the string length when you create the type. HDF5 supports fixed-length strings natively:

```
>>> dt = np.dtype("S10")  # 10-character byte string
>>> dset = f.create_dataset('fixed_string', (100,), dtype=dt)
>>> dset[0] = "Hello"
>>> dset[0]
'Hello'
```

Like NumPy fixed-width strings, HDF5 will truncate strings that are too big:

```
>>> dset[0] = "thisstringhasmorethan10characters"
>>> dset[0]
'thisstring'
```

Technically, these are fixed-length *byte* strings, which means they use one byte per character. In HDF5, they are assumed to store ASCII text only. NumPy also supports fixed-width Unicode strings, which use multiple bytes to store each character and can represent things outside the ASCII range. The NumPy dtype for this is kind "U," as in dtype("U10").

Unfortunately, HDF5 does not support such "wide-character" Unicode strings, so there's no way to directly store "U" strings in a file. However, you aren't out of luck on the Unicode front. First, we'll have to take a detour and discuss one of the best features in HDF5: variable-length strings.

Variable-Length Strings

If you've used NumPy for a while, you're used to one subtle but important aspect of its design: all elements in an array *have the same size*. There are a lot of advantages to this design; for example, to locate the 115th element of a dataset containing 4-byte floats, you know to look 460 bytes from the beginning of the array. And most types you use in everyday computation are of a fixed size—once you've chosen to work with double-precision floats, for example, they're all 8 bytes wide.

This begins to break down when you come to string types. As we saw earlier, NumPy natively includes two string types: one 8-bit "ASCII" string type and one 32-bit "Unicode" string type. You have to explicitly set the size of the string when you create the type. For example, let's create a length-3 ASCII string array and initialize it:

```
>>> dt = np.dtype('S3')
>>> a = np.array( [ "a", "ab", "abc", "abcd" ], dtype=dt)
>>> a
array(['a', 'ab', 'abc', 'abc'],
      dtype='|S3')
```

The limitation is obvious: elements with more than three characters are simply truncated, and the information is lost. It's tempting to simply increase the length of the string type, say to 100, or 256. But we end up wasting a lot of memory, and there's still no guarantee our guess will be large enough:

```
# Read first 5 lines from file
# Ed M. 4/3/12: Increased max line size from 100 to 256 per issue #344
# Ed M. 5/1/12: Increased to 1000 per issue #345
# Ed M. 6/2/12: Fixed.
# TODO: mysterious crashes with MemoryError when many threads running (#346)

a = np.empty((5,), dtype='S100000')
for idx in xrange(5):
    a[idx] = textfile.readline()
```

This isn't a problem in every application, of course. But there's no getting around the fact that strings in real-world data can have virtually any length.

Fortunately, HDF5 has a mechanism to handle this: *variable-length strings*. Like native Python strings (and strings in C), these can be any width that fits in memory. Here's how to take advantage of them.

The vlen String Data Type

First, since NumPy doesn't support variable-length strings at all, we need to use a special dtype provided by h5py:

```
>>> dt = h5py.special_dtype(vlen=str)
>>> dt
dtype(('|O4', [(({'type': <type 'str'>}, 'vlen'), '|O4')]))
```

That looks like a mess. But it's actually a standard NumPy dtype with some metadata attached. In this case, the underlying type is the NumPy *object* dtype:

```
>>> dt.kind
'O'
```

NumPy arrays of kind "O" hold ordinary Python objects. So the dtype effectively says, "This is an object array, which is intended to hold Python strings."

Depending on your version of h5py, you may see a different result when you print the dtype; the details of how the "special" data is attached vary. Don't depend on any specific implementation. Always use the special_dtype function and don't try to piece one together yourself.

Working with vlen String Datasets

You can use a "special" dtype to create an array in the normal fashion. Here we create a 100-element variable-length string dataset:

```
>>> dset = f.create_dataset('vlen_dataset', (100,), dtype=dt)
```

You can write strings into it from anything that looks "string-shaped," including ordinary Python strings and fixed-length NumPy strings:

```
>>> dset[0] = "Hello"
>>> dset[1] = np.string_("Hello2")
>>> dset[3] = "X"*10000
```

Retrieving a single element, you get a Python string:

```
>>> out = dset[0]
>>> type(out)
str
```

Retrieving more than one, you get an object array full of Python strings:

```
>>> dset[0:2]
array([Hello, Hello2], dtype=object)
```

There's one caveat here: for technical reasons, the array returned has a plain-vanilla "object" dtype, not the fancy dtype we created from h5py.special_dtype:

```
>>> out = dset[0:1]
>>> out.dtype
dtype('object')
```

This is one of very few cases where dset[...].dtype != dset.dtype.

Byte Versus Unicode Strings

The preceding examples, like the rest of this book, are written assuming you are using Python 2. However, in both Python 2 and 3 there exist two "flavors" of string you should be aware of. They are stored in the file slightly differently, and this has implications for both internationalized applications and data portability.

A complete discussion of the bytes/Unicode mess in Python is beyond the scope of this book. However, it's important to discuss how the two types interact with HDF5.

The Python 2 `str` type, used earlier, is more properly called a *byte string* in the Python world. As the name implies, these are sequences of single-byte elements. They're available on both Python 2 and 3 under the name `bytes` (it's a simple alias for `str` on Python 2, and a separate type on Python 3). They're intended to hold strictly binary strings, although in the Python 2 world they play a dual role, generally representing ASCII or Latin-1 encoded text.

In the HDF5 world, these represent "ASCII" strings. Although no checking is done, they are expected to contain values in the range 0-127 and represent plain-ASCII text. When you create a dataset on Python 2 using:

```
>>> h5py.special_dtype(vlen=str)
```

or the equivalent-but-more-readable:

```
>>> h5py.special_dtype(vlen=bytes)
```

the underlying dataset is created with an ASCII character set. Since there are many third-party applications for HDF5 that understand only ASCII strings, this is by far the most compatible configuration.

Using Unicode Strings

The Python 2 `unicode` type properly represents "text" strings, in contrast to the `str`/`bytes` "byte" strings just discussed. On Python 3, "byte" strings are called `bytes` and the equivalent "text" strings are called—wait for it—`str`. Wonderful.

These strings hold sequences of more abstract Unicode *characters*. You're not supposed to worry about how they're actually represented. Before you can store them somewhere, you need to explicitly *encode* them, which means translating them into byte sequences. The rules that translate these "text" strings into byte strings are called *encodings*. HDF5 uses the UTF-8 encoding, which is very space-efficient for strings that contain mainly Western characters.

You can actually store these "Unicode" or "text" strings directly in HDF5, by using a similar "special" dtype:

```
>>> dt = h5py.special_dtype(vlen=unicode)
>>> dt
dtype(('|O4', [(({'type': <type 'unicode'>}, 'vlen'), '|O4')]))
```

Like before, you can create datasets and interact with them. But now you can use non-ASCII characters:

```
>>> dset = f.create_dataset('vlen_unicode', (100,), dtype=dt)
>>> dset[0] = "Hello"
>>> dset[1] = u"Accent: \u00E9"
>>> dset[0]
u'Hello'
>>> dset[1]
```

```
u'Accent: \xe9'
>>> print dset[1]
Accent: é
```

When you create this kind of a dataset, the underlying HDF5 character set is set to "UTF-8." The only disadvantage is that some older third-party applications, like IDL, may not be able to read your strings. If compatibility with legacy code like this is essential for your application, make sure you test!

 Remember the default string on Python 3, str, is actually a Unicode string. So on Python 3, h5py.special_dtype(vlen=str) will give you a UTF-8 dataset, not the compatible-with-everything ASCII dataset. Use vlen=bytes instead to get an ASCII dataset.

Don't Store Binary Data in Strings!

Finally, note that HDF5 will allow you to store raw binary data using the "ASCII" dataset dtype created with special_dtype(vlen=bytes). This may work, but is generally considered evil. And because of how the strings are handled internally, if your binary string has NULLs in it ("\x00"), it will be silently truncated!

The best way to store raw binary data is with the "opaque" type (see "Opaque Types" on page 98).

Future-Proofing Your Python 2 Application

Finally, here are some simple rules you can follow to keep the bytes/Unicode mess from driving you mad. They will also help you when porting to Python 3, using the context-free translation tool 2to3 that ships with Python.

1. Keep the text-versus-bytes distinction clear in your mind, and cleanly separate the two in code.

2. Always use the alias bytes instead of str when you're sure you want a byte string. For literals, you can even use the "b" prefix, for example, b"Hello". In particular, when calling special_dtype to create a byte string, *always* use bytes.

3. For text strings use str, or better yet, unicode. Unicode literals are entered with a leading "u": u"Hello".

Compound Types

For some kinds of data, it makes sense to bundle closely related values together into a single element. The classic example is a C struct: multiple pieces of data that are handled together but can individually be accessed. Another example would be tables in a SQL-style database or a CSV file with multiple column names; each element of data (a row) consists of several related pieces of data (the column values).

NumPy supports this feature through *structured arrays*, which are similar to (but not the same as) the recarray class. The dtype for these arrays contains a series of *fields*, each of which has a name and its own sub-dtype. Here's an example: suppose we wanted to store 100 data elements from a weather-monitoring experiment, which periodically gives us values for temperature, pressure, and wind speed:

```
>>> dt = np.dtype([("temp", np.float), ("pressure", np.float), ("wind",
np.float)])
>>> a = np.zeros((100,), dtype=dt)
```

In NumPy, you can use a single field name (e.g., "temp") as an index, which in this example would return a shape-(100,) array of floats:

```
>>> out = a["temp"]
>>> out.shape
(100,)
>>> out.dtype
dtype('float64')
```

When you access a single element, you get back an object that supports dictionary-style access on the field names:

```
>>> out = a[0]
>>> out
(0.0, 0.0, 0.0)
>>> out["temp"]
0.0
```

With HDF5, you have a little more flexibility. Let's use the same dtype to create a dataset in our file:

```
>>> dset = f.create_dataset("compound", (100,), dtype=dt)
```

You're not limited to a single field when slicing into the dataset. We can access both the "temp" and pressure fields:

```
>>> out = dset["temp","pressure"]
>>> out.shape
(100,)
>>> out.dtype
dtype([('temp', '<f8'), ('pressure', '<f8')])
```

We can even mix field names and slices, for example to retrieve only the last 10 temperature points:

```
>>> out = dset["temp", 90:100]
>>> out.shape
(10,)
```

```
>>> out.dtype
dtype('float64')
```

This process is very efficient; HDF5 only reads the fields you request from disk. Likewise, you can choose to "update" only those fields you wish. If we were to set all the temperatures we just read to a new value and write back out:

```
>>> out[...] = 98.6
>>> dset["temp", 90:100] = out
```

HDF5 updates only the `temp` field in each record. So if, for example, you want to modify only the temperature or pressure part of the dataset, you can cut your memory use by a factor of three.

Complex Numbers

Both NumPy and Python itself support *complex numbers*. These objects consist of two floating-point numbers pasted together, one representing the real part, and one the imaginary part of the number. In NumPy, you can have single precision (8 bytes total), double precision (16 bytes total), or extended precision (24 bytes total):

```
>>> dset = f.create_dataset('single_complex', (100,), dtype='c8')
```

While HDF5 has no out-of-the-box representation for complex numbers, a standard of sorts has arisen, to which h5py adheres. Complex numbers are stored as a two-element compound, the real part labelled *r*, and the imaginary part labelled *i*. Keep this in mind if you want to access the data in other programs like IDL or MATLAB. Here's what the dataset we created looks like with `h5ls`:

```
Opened "test.hdf5" with sec2 driver.
/                       Group
    Location:  1:96
    Links:     1
/single_complex         Dataset {100/100}
    Location:  1:800
    Links:     1
    Storage:   800 logical bytes, 0 allocated bytes
    Type:      struct {
                   "r"              +0      native float
                   "i"              +4      native float
               } 8 bytes
```

Enumerated Types

Those of you who have used C will recognize this next datatype. In the HDF5 world, *enumerated types* or *enums* are integer datatypes for which certain values are associated with text tags. For example, for a dataset of type `np.uint8` you might define 0 to mean RED, 1 to mean GREEN, and 2 to mean BLUE.

The point of all this is to store the "semantic" meaning of these values as close as possible to the data itself, rather than, for example, in Appendix G of a manual that nobody reads.

There's no native concept for this in the NumPy world, so we fall back again to our friend h5py.special_dtype. In this case, we use a different keyword, enum, and supply both a base type and dictionary mapping names to values:

```
>>> mapping = {"RED": 0, "GREEN": 1, "BLUE": 2}
>>> dt = h5py.special_dtype( enum=(np.int8, mapping) )
```

Datasets you create with this type work just like regular integer datasets:

```
>>> dset = f.create_dataset('enum', (100,), dtype=dt)
>>> dset[0]
0
```

Like variable-length strings, data you read from the dataset will have the extra "special dtype" information stripped off:

```
>>> dset[0].dtype
dtype('int8')
```

Keep in mind that in both HDF5 and NumPy, no checking is performed to make sure you keep to values specified in the enum. For example, if you were to assign one element to a different value, HDF5 will happily store it:

```
>>> dset[0] = 100
>>> dset[0]
100
```

It's strictly on the honor system.

 HDF5 itself doesn't like to convert between integers and enums. So if you create an enum dataset, keep in mind that people who read your data will have to explicitly read it as an enum. Generally this works fine, but as always, if you're interacting with third-party code it's a good idea to test.

Booleans

When storing Boolean (True/False) flags, people often resort to simply using integers. In Chapter 3, we saw that NumPy natively supports arrays of Booleans. They have their own data type, np.bool. NumPy hides the storage type from you, but behind the scenes, arrays of type bool are stored as single-byte integers.

There's no native HDF5 Boolean type, but like complex numbers, h5py automatically provides one for you (in this case using an enum). The base type is np.int8 and the mapping is {"FALSE": 0, "TRUE": 1}. Let's create a Boolean dataset:

```
>>> with h5py.File('bool.hdf5','w') as f2:
...     f.create_dataset('bool', (100,), dtype=np.bool)
```

And now let's see how it looks in the file, again using h5ls:

```
Opened "bool.hdf5" with sec2 driver.
/                              Group
    Location:   1:96
    Links:      1
/bool                          Dataset {100/100}
    Location:   1:800
    Links:      1
    Storage:    100 logical bytes, 0 allocated bytes
    Type:       enum native signed char {
                    FALSE            = 0
                    TRUE             = 1
                }
```

The array Type

Not often encountered in NumPy code, the *array* type is a good choice when you want to store multiple values of the same type in a single element. Unlike compound types, there are no separate "fields"; rather, each element is itself a multidimensional array.

There are a couple of pitfalls associated with this type and with some "helpful" behavior from NumPy, which can be confusing. Let's start with an example, in which our elements are 2×2 arrays of floats:

```
>>> dt = np.dtype('(2,2)f')
>>> dt
dtype(('float32',(2, 2)))
```

Now let's create an HDF5 dataset with this dtype that has 100 data points:

```
>>> dset = f.create_dataset('array', (100,), dtype=dt)
>>> dset.dtype
dtype(('float32',(2, 2)))
>>> dset.shape
(100,)
```

Retrieving a single element gives us a 2x2 NumPy array:

```
>>> out = dset[0]
>>> out
array([[ 0.,  0.],
       [ 0.,  0.]], dtype=float32)
```

You might have expected a NumPy scalar with our original dtype, but it doesn't work that way. NumPy automatically "promotes" the array-type scalar into a full-fledged array of the base type. This is convenient, but it's another case where dset[...].dtype != dset.dtype.

Likewise, if we were to create a native NumPy array with our type it would get "eaten" and the extra axes tacked on to the main array's shape:

```
>>> a = np.zeros((100,), dtype=dt)
>>> a.dtype
dtype('float32')
>>> a.shape
(100, 2, 2)
```

So what's the array type good for? Generally it's best used as an element of a compound type. For example, if we had an experiment that reported an integer timestamp along with the output from a 2×2 light sensor, one choice for a data type would be:

```
>>> dt_timestamp = np.dtype('uint64')
>>> dt_sensor = np.dtype('(2,2)f')
>>> dt = np.dtype([ ('time', dt_timestamp), ('sensor', dt_sensor) ])
```

Creating a dataset with this compound type, it's easy to store and retrieve individual outputs from the experiment:

```
>>> import time
>>> dset = f.create_dataset('mydata', (100,), dtype=dt)
>>> dset["time", 0] = time.time()
>>> dset["sensor", 0] = ((1,2), (3,4))
>>> out = dset[0]
>>> out
(1368217143, [[1.0, 2.0], [3.0, 4.0]])
>>> out["sensor"]
array([[ 1.,   2.],
       [ 3.,   4.]], dtype=float32)
```

When your data contains "packets" of values like this, it's generally better to use the array type than, say, add extra dimensions to the dataset. Not only does it make access easier, but it's semantically more meaningful.

Opaque Types

It's rare, but some data simply can't be represented in any of the NumPy forms (for example, disk images or other binary data that isn't numeric). There's a mechanism for dealing with this in HDF5, which you should consider a last resort for data that needs to be stored, bit for bit, in the file.

The NumPy *void* "V" type is used to store such "opaque" data. Like the string type "S" this is a fixed-width flexible type. For example, to store opaque fields 200 bytes long in NumPy:

```
>>> dt = np.dtype('V200')
>>> a = np.zeros((10,), dtype=dt)  # 10 elements each 200 bytes long
```

When you provide such a dtype to `create_dataset`, the underlying dataset is created with the HDF5 opaque datatype:

```
>>> dset = f.create_dataset('opaque', (10,), dtype=dt)
>>> dset.dtype
dtype('|V200')
>>> dset.shape
(10,)
```

You should seriously consider using opaque types for storing raw binary data. It may be tempting simply to store the data in a string, but remember that strings in HDF5 are reserved either for ASCII or Unicode text.

Here's an example of how to "round-trip" a Python byte string through the HDF5 opaque type, in this case to store binary data in an attribute:

```
>>> binary_blob = b"A\x00B\x00"      # Try storing this directly! It won't work.
>>> obj.attrs["name"] = np.void(binary_blob)  # "Void" type maps to HDF5 opaque
>>> out = obj.attrs["name"]
>>> binary_blob = out.tostring()
```

Dates and Times

One frequently asked question is how to express time information in HDF5. At one point there was a datetime type in HDF5, although to my knowledge nobody in the Python world ever used it. Typically dates and times are expressed in HDF5 on an ad-hoc basis.

One way to represent time is by a count of seconds (including fractional seconds) since some time in the past, called the "epoch." For example, "Unix time" or "POSIX time" counts the number of seconds since midnight Jan. 1, 1970 UTC.

If you need only seconds of resolution, an integer works well:

```
>>> timestamp = np.dtype('u8')
```

You can also use a double-precision float to represent fractional time, as provided by the built-in time.time():

```
>>> import time, datetime
>>> time.time()
1377548506.627
```

datetime objects can be used to provide a string in "ISO" format, which yields a nicer-looking result:

```
>>> datetime.datetime.now().isoformat()
'2013-08-26T14:30:02.633000'
```

Such timestamps are also called "naive" timestamps, because they don't include information on the time zone or leap seconds. If your application is purely working in one time zone, or only dealing in time differences (and can ignore leap seconds for this purpose), this is likely OK. Otherwise, you will have to store appropriate data on the time zone somewhere close by (like in another member of a compound type).

There's one last type to discuss, and it's important enough to warrant its own chapter in this book. We have come to references: the HDF5 pointer type.

## CHAPTER 8

Organizing Data with References, Types, and Dimension Scales

Your files aren't just a collection of groups, datasets, and attributes. Some of the best features in HDF5 are those that help you to express relationships between pieces of your data.

Maybe one of your datasets provides the x-axis for another, and you'd like to express that in a way your colleagues can easily figure out. Maybe you want to record which regions of a particular dataset are of interest for further processing. Or maybe you just want to store a bunch of links to datasets and groups in the file, without having to worry about getting all the paths right.

This chapter covers three of the most useful constructs in HDF5 for linking your various objects together into a scientifically useful whole. References, the HDF5 "pointer" type, are a great way to store links to objects as data. Named types let you enforce type consistency across datasets. And Dimension Scales, an HDF5 standard, let you attach physically meaningful axes to your data in a way third-party programs can understand.

Let's get started with the simplest relational widget in HDF5: object references.

Object References

We've already seen how links in a group serve to locate objects. But there's another mechanism that can do this, and crucially, this kind can be stored as data in things like attributes and datasets.

Creating and Resolving References

Let's create a simple file with a couple of groups and a dataset:

```
>>> f = h5py.File('refs_demo.hdf5','w')
>>> grp1 = f.create_group('group1')
>>> grp2 = f.create_group('group2')
>>> dset = f.create_dataset('mydata', shape=(100,))
```

Looking at the group grp1, we notice an interesting property called ref:

```
>>> grp1.ref
<HDF5 object reference>
```

The object returned from accessing .ref is an HDF5 *object reference*. These are basically pointers to objects in the file. You can "dereference" them by using the same syntax as we used for string names:

```
>>> out = f[grp1.ref]
>>> out == grp1
True
```

By the way, the Python type for these objects is available at h5py.Reference, in case you want to use isinstance:

```
>>> isinstance(grp1.ref, h5py.Reference)
True
```

Since the reference is an "absolute" way of locating an object, you can use any group in the file for dereferencing, not just the root group:

```
>>> out = grp2[grp1.ref]
>>> out == grp1
True
```

But keep in mind they're local to the file. Trying to dereference them in the context of another file will fail:

```
>>> with h5py.File('anotherfile.hdf5','w') as f2:
...     out = f2[grp1.ref]
ValueError: unable dereference object
```

References as "Unbreakable" Links

So far there seems to be no improvement over using links. But there's an important difference: you can store them as *data*, and they're independent of later renaming of the objects involved.

Here's an example: suppose we wanted to add an attribute on one of our groups pointing to the dataset mydata. We could simply record the name as an attribute:

```
>>> grp1.attrs['dataset'] = dset.name
>>> grp1.attrs['dataset']
u'/mydata'
>>> out = f[grp1.attrs['dataset']]
>>> out == dset
True
```

But if we rename the dataset, this quickly breaks:

```
>>> f.move('mydata', 'mydata2')
>>> out = f[grp1.attrs['dataset']]
KeyError: "unable to open object"
```

Using object references instead, we have:

```
>>> grp1.attrs['dataset'] = dset.ref
>>> grp1.attrs['dataset']
<HDF5 object reference>
>>> out = f[grp1.attrs['dataset']]
>>> out == dset
True
```

Moving the dataset yet again, the reference still resolves:

```
>>> f.move('mydata2','mydata3')
>>> out = f[grp1.attrs['dataset']]
>>> out == dset
True
```

 When you open an object by dereferencing, every now and then it's possible that HDF5 won't be able to figure out the object's name. In that case, obj.name will return None. It's less of a problem than it used to be (HDF5 1.8 has gotten very good at figuring out names), but don't be alarmed if you happen to get None.

References as Data

References are full-fledged types in HDF5; you can freely use them in both attributes and datasets. Obviously there's no native type in NumPy for references, so we once again call on special_dtype for help, this time with the ref keyword:

```
>>> dt = h5py.special_dtype(ref=h5py.Reference)
>>> dt
dtype(('|O4', [((({'type': <type 'h5py.h5r.Reference'>}, 'ref'), '|O4')]))
```

That's a lot of metadata. But don't be dismayed; just like variable-length strings, this is otherwise a regular object dtype:

```
>>> dt.kind
'O'
```

We can easily create datasets of Reference type:

```
>>> ref_dset = f.create_dataset("references", (10,), dtype=dt)
```

What's in such a dataset? If we retrieve an uninitialized element, we get a zeroed or "null" reference:

```
>>> out = ref_dset[0]
>>> out
<HDF5 object reference (null)>
```

Like a null pointer in C, this reference doesn't point to anything. Like trying to dereference against the wrong file, dereferencing a null reference just results in `ValueError`:

```
>>> f[out]
ValueError: Invalid HDF5 object reference
```

There's a simple way to check for a null reference, without having to catch exceptions.
The truth value of a reference indicates whether or not it's null:

```
>>> bool(out)
False
>>> bool(grp1.ref)
True
```

 Keep in mind that a value of `True` *doesn't* mean that the reference
actually resolves to something, just that it isn't null. If, for example, you
create a reference and then delete the object, the reference will evalu-
ate as `True` but you will still get `ValueError` when you attempt to
dereference it.

Region References

Region references are one of the coolest features of HDF5. These let you store a reference
to *part* of a dataset. For example, you might want to store a region of interest (ROI) on
photographs stored in an HDF5 file, so that during later analysis you don't have to
process the whole thing.

Creating Region References and Reading

You can think of region references as effectively *storing your slicing arguments* for dataset
access. Here's an example: looking at the dataset created in the previous example, we
notice a property named `regionref`:

```
>>> dset.name
u'/mydata3'
>>> dset.shape
(100,)
>>> dset.regionref
<h5py._hl.dataset._RegionProxy at 0x459d6d0>
```

This is a little proxy object which we can use to store our selections. You create a new
region reference by applying the standard NumPy slicing syntax to this object:

```
>>> ref_out = dset.regionref[10:90]
>>> ref_out
<HDF5 region reference>
```

Like object references, region references are generally opaque. The only useful aspects are the shape of the dataspace (the same as the parent dataset), and the shape of your selection:

```
>>> dset.regionref.shape(ref_out)(100,)
>>> dset.regionref.selection(ref_out)(80,)
```

This represents the shape of your selection; in other words, if you had applied your slicing arguments directly to the dataset, it's the shape of the array that would have been returned from HDF5.

Once you've got a region reference, you can use it directly as a slicing argument to retrieve data from the dataset:

```
>>> data = dset[ref_out]
>>> data
array([ 0.,  0.,  0.,  0.,  0.,  0.,  0.,  0.,  0.,  0.,  0.,  0.,  0.,
        0.,  0.,  0.,  0.,  0.,  0.,  0.,  0.,  0.,  0.,  0.,  0.,  0.,
        0.,  0.,  0.,  0.,  0.,  0.,  0.,  0.,  0.,  0.,  0.,  0.,  0.,
        0.,  0.,  0.,  0.,  0.,  0.,  0.,  0.,  0.,  0.,  0.,  0.,  0.,
        0.,  0.,  0.,  0.,  0.,  0.,  0.,  0.,  0.,  0.,  0.,  0.,  0.,
        0.,  0.,  0.,  0.,  0.,  0.,  0.,  0.,  0.,  0.,  0.,  0.,  0.,
        0.,  0.], dtype=float32)
>>> data.shape
(80,)
```

Fancy Indexing

Keep in mind that if you're using "fancy" indexing methods (like Boolean arrays), then the shape will *always* be one-dimensional. This mimics the behavior of NumPy for such selections.

For example, suppose we had a little two-dimensional array, which we populated with some random numbers:

```
>>> dset_random = f.create_dataset('small_example', (3,3))
>>> dset_random[...] = np.random.random((3,3))
>>> dset_random[...]
array([[ 0.32391435,  0.070962  ,  0.57038087],
       [ 0.1530778 ,  0.22476801,  0.7758832 ],
       [ 0.75768745,  0.73156554,  0.3228527 ]], dtype=float32)
```

We could create a Boolean array representing the entries greater than 0.5:

```
>>> index_arr = dset_random[...] > 0.5
>>> index_arr
array([[False, False,  True],
```

```
            [False, False,  True],
            [ True,  True, False]], dtype=bool)
```

You can create a region reference from this array:

```
>>> random_ref = dset_random.regionref[index_arr]
>>> dset_random.regionref.selection(random_ref)
(4,)
```

There were a total of four elements that matched, so the selection result is "packed" into a four-element 1D buffer.

There is a rule to the order in which such elements are retrieved. If we apply our selection to the dataset:

```
>>> data = dset_random[random_ref]
>>> data
array([ 0.57038087,  0.7758832 ,  0.75768745,  0.73156554], dtype=float32)
```

Looking closely, it appears that the elements retrieved are at [0,2], [1,2], [2,0], [2,1], in that order. You'll recognize this as "C" order; the selection advances through the last index, then the next to last, and so on.

 Unfortunately, list-based selections will also be returned as 1D arrays, unlike NumPy (try it!). This is a limitation of the HDF5 library.

Finding Datasets with Region References

There's one more trick region references can do. If you have a region reference, say our shape-(80,) selection ref_out from earlier, you can use it as an object reference to retrieve the dataset:

```
>>> f[ref_out]
<HDF5 dataset "mydata3": shape (100,), type "<f4">
```

This can come in handy when you've stored a region reference as an attribute somewhere. It means you don't have to also store an object reference to figure out where to apply the selection.

And if you're just after the data and don't care about the dataset itself, all you have to do is:

```
>>> selected_data = f[ref_out][ref_out]
```

Named Types

There's one more "linking" concept in HDF5, and it's much more subtle than either object or region references. We've already seen that when you create a dataset (or an attribute), it's created with a fixed data type. Suppose you have multiple data products in a file (for example, many datasets containing image data), and you want to be sure each has exactly the same type.

HDF5 provides a native way to ensure this, by allowing you to save a data type to the file *independently* of any particular dataset or attribute. When you call `create_data set`, you supply the stored type and HDF5 will "link" the type to the brand new dataset.

The Datatype Object

You can create such an independent, or "named" type, by simply assigning a NumPy dtype to a name in the file:

```
>>> f['mytype'] = np.dtype('float32')
```

When we open the named type, we don't get a dtype back, but something else:

```
>>> out = f['mytype']
>>> out
<HDF5 named type "mytype" (dtype <f4)>
```

Like the `Dataset` object, this `h5py.Datatype` object is a thin proxy that allows access to the underlying HDF5 datatype. The most immediately obvious property is `Data type.dtype`, which returns the equivalent NumPy dtype object:

```
>>> out.dtype
dtype('float32')
```

Since they're full-fledged objects in the file, you have a lot of other properties as well:

```
>>> out.name
u'/mytype'
>>> out.parent
<HDF5 group "/" (6 members)>
```

Also available are `.file` (`h5py.File` instance containing the type), `.ref` (object reference to the type), and attributes, just like `Dataset` and `Group` objects:

```
>>> out.attrs['info'] = "This is an attribute on a named type object"
```

 In the HDF5 world, for technical reasons named types are now called *committed types*. You may hear both terms; for our purposes, they mean the same thing.

Linking to Named Types

It's simple to create a dataset or attribute that refers to a named type object; just supply the `Datatype` instance as the dtype:

```
>>> dset = f.create_dataset("typedemo", (100,), dtype=f['mytype'])
```

When you do this, HDF5 doesn't copy the type into the dataset; it actually makes a reference to the named type object elsewhere in the file. So on top of helping you keep data organized, it saves disk space as well.

For attributes, remember you'll have to explicitly supply the type via the `create` method. For example, to create an attribute on the root group that uses our named type:

```
>>> f.attrs.create("attribute_demo", 1.0, dtype=f['mytype'])
```

Managing Named Types

You can't modify named types once they're created, although you can unlink them from the file:

```
>>> del f['mytype']
```

But don't try to trick HDF5 by replacing it with a new, different type. The stored type information can't be unlinked from the datasets and attributes that point to it. It'll hang around in the shadows until every dataset and attribute that used it is deleted from the file:

```
>>> f['mytype'] = np.dtype('int16')
>>> dset = f['typedemo']
>>> dset.dtype
dtype('float32')
```

Dimension Scales

Real-world data comes with units attached. Suppose we have a 3D dataset that is the output from an atmospheric simulation, representing temperatures at various points within a volume:

```
>>> dset = f.create_dataset('temperatures', (100,100,100), dtype='f')
```

It's easy enough to recognize that dataset records "temperature"—we could even add an attribute to record the scale:

```
>>> dset.attrs['temp_units'] = "C"
```

But there's a more subtle problem. Suppose our simulation is focused on a convection process, and has much greater resolution in the z direction than either the x or y directions; for example, the steps in the vertical direction might be 100 meters while the steps in the horizontal direction might be 10 kilometers. We could add more attributes, perhaps by having a "step" attribute like so:

```
>>> dset.attrs['steps'] = [10000,10000,100]
```

By the way, which axis is which? Does the first axis represent the x direction, as we might expect? Or does the simulation output z first? We could add another attribute, I guess, which records this:

```
>>> dset.attrs['axes'] = ["x", "y", "z"]
```

We would have to tell all of our colleagues about this convention, of course, and it would look "squished" in viewers that don't know about our ad hoc naming convention, and I suppose if we change to variable-sized steps in the *z* direction it would break...

It turns out this situation is common enough that a standard has arisen: the HDF5 *Dimension Scales* specification. Like the ad hoc system of attributes earlier, it's a feature built *on top* of HDF5, using the machinery of datasets, attributes, and references in a standardized way to build a more expressive object.

There are a lot of features like this, all standardized by the HDF Group (authors and maintainers of the HDF5 software suite) in a series of RFCs. The big advantage of this approach is that third-party applications know what to do with certain specific combinations of groups, datasets, attributes, and references. For example, a viewer program would render our simulation "unsquished" by honoring the axes we create. Or, in the case of the HDF5 *Image* standard, the viewer could determine the appropriate palette to render an astronomical photograph.

Creating Dimension Scales

Let's revisit our dataset with 3D temperature measurements. First, we'll erase the attributes we applied, before using Dimension Scales to do it right:

```
>>> for name in dset.attrs:
...     del dset.attrs[name]
```

There's a property attached to our dataset, which up until now we've ignored:

```
>>> dset.dims
<Dimensions of HDF5 object at 74374048>
```

This is our entry point for Dimension Scales. In HDF5, a "dimension scale" is a separate "axis" dataset with some metadata, linked to the main dataset using references. In our example, we want to create three dimension scales: one for *x*, with steps of 10 km, one for *y*, also with steps of 10 km, and one for *z*, in steps of 100 m.

To record this, we first create three datasets in the file which will hold our Dimension Scale "axes":

```
>>> f.create_dataset('scale_x', data=np.arange(100)*10e3)
>>> f.create_dataset('scale_y', data=np.arange(100)*10e3)
>>> f.create_dataset('scale_z', data=np.arange(100)*100.0)
```

Now, we ask HDF5 to turn them into official "Dimension Scale" datasets by using the `create_scale` method on `dset.dims`:

```
>>> dset.dims.create_scale(f['scale_x'], "Simulation X (North) axis")
>>> dset.dims.create_scale(f['scale_y'], "Simulation Y (East) axis")
>>> dset.dims.create_scale(f['scale_z'], "Simulation Z (Vertical) axis")
```

It's worth taking a moment to see what actually happens when we do this. Let's inspect the attributes of the `scale_x` dataset and see what's there:

```
>>> for key, val in f['scale_x'].attrs.iteritems():
...     print key, ':', val
CLASS : DIMENSION_SCALE
NAME : Simulation X (North) axis
```

That's really it. All `create_scale` did was attach a few attributes with standardized names and values.

Attaching Scales to a Dataset

Now that we have our three scales, we can associate them with our dataset. Note, however, that we have to associate each scale with a particular axis of the dataset. This is expressed by using indexing on the `Dataset.dims` object:

```
>>> dset.dims[0].attach_scale(f['scale_x'])
>>> dset.dims[1].attach_scale(f['scale_y'])
>>> dset.dims[2].attach_scale(f['scale_z'])
```

The object at `dims[N]` is yet another little proxy, in this case keeping track of which dimension scales are attached to the first axis of the dataset. Yes, you can have multiple scales attached to a single axis! Good news for those of you who create plots with an axis on every side.

The `dims[N]` proxy works like an ordered dictionary and supports access by both name and index. In this case, the index refers to the order in which scales were added. For example, to get the dataset containing our *x* scale, we could ask for the first scale associated with dimension 0 of the dataset:

```
>>> dset.dims[0][0]
<HDF5 dataset "scale_x": shape (100,), type "<f8">
```

And to get the actual axis values, simply slice into the dataset:

```
>>> dset.dims[0][0][...]
array([      0.,    10000.,    20000.,    30000.,    40000.,    50000.,
         60000.,    70000.,    80000.,    90000.,   100000.,   110000.,
        120000.,   130000.,   140000.,   150000.,   160000.,   170000.,
        180000.,   190000.,   200000.,   210000.,   220000.,   230000.,
        240000.,   250000.,   260000.,   270000.,   280000.,   290000.,
        300000.,   310000.,   320000.,   330000.,   340000.,   350000.,
        360000.,   370000.,   380000.,   390000.,   400000.,   410000.,
        420000.,   430000.,   440000.,   450000.,   460000.,   470000.,
        480000.,   490000.,   500000.,   510000.,   520000.,   530000.,
        540000.,   550000.,   560000.,   570000.,   580000.,   590000.,
        600000.,   610000.,   620000.,   630000.,   640000.,   650000.,
        660000.,   670000.,   680000.,   690000.,   700000.,   710000.,
        720000.,   730000.,   740000.,   750000.,   760000.,   770000.,
        780000.,   790000.,   800000.,   810000.,   820000.,   830000.,
```

```
840000., 850000., 860000., 870000., 880000., 890000.,
900000., 910000., 920000., 930000., 940000., 950000.,
960000., 970000., 980000., 990000.])
```

We could also use dictionary-style access using the name we supplied when creating the scale:

```
>>> dset.dims[0]["Simulation X (North) axis"]
<HDF5 dataset "scale_x": shape (100,), type "<f8">
```

There are a couple of other dictionary-like methods too, including items, keys, and values.

Finally, you can label each axis of the dataset. This is the correct place to record which axis is *x, y, z*, etc.:

```
>>> dset.dims[0].label = "x"
>>> dset.dims[1].label = "y"
>>> dset.dims[2].label = "z"
```

Now that we've covered all the basic constructs, it's time to talk about one of the thorniest issues when programming with HDF5: concurrency.

## CHAPTER 9

Concurrency: Parallel HDF5, Threading, and Multiprocessing

Over the past 10 years or so, parallel code has become crucial to scientific programming. Nearly every modern computer has at least two cores; dedicated workstations are readily available with 12 or more. Plunging hardware prices have made 100-core clusters feasible even for small research groups.

As a rapid development language, and one with easy access to C and FORTRAN libraries, Python is increasingly being used as a top-level "glue" language for such platforms. Scientific programs written in Python can leverage existing "heavy-lifting" libraries written in C or FORTRAN using any number of mechanisms, from `ctypes` to Cython to the built-in NumPy routines.

This chapter discusses the various mechanisms in Python for writing parallel code, and how they interact with HDF5.

Python Parallel Basics

Broadly speaking, there are three ways to do concurrent programming in Python: threads, the `multiprocessing` module, and finally by using bindings for the Message Passing Interface (MPI).

Thread-based code is fine for GUIs and applications that call into external libraries that don't tie up the Python interpreter. As we'll see in a moment, you can't use more than one core's worth of time when running a pure-Python program. There's also no performance advantage on the HDF5 side to using threads, since the HDF5 library serializes all calls.

`multiprocessing` is a more recent built-in module available with Python, which provides support for basic `fork()`-based parallel processing. The main restriction is that your parallel processes can't share a single HDF5 file, even if the file is opened read-only. This is a limitation of the HDF5 library. `multiprocessing`-based code is great for long-running, CPU-bound problems in which data I/O is a relatively small component handled by the master process. It's the simplest way in Python to write parallel code that uses more than one core, and strongly recommended for general-purpose computation.

For anything else, MPI-based Parallel HDF5 is by far the best way to go. MPI is the official "flavor" of parallelism supported by the HDF5 library. You can have an unlimited number of processes, all of which share the same open HDF5 file. All of them can read and write data, and modify the file's structure. Programs written this way require a little more care, but it's the most elegant and highest-performance way to use HDF5 in a parallel context.

By the way, there's even a fourth mechanism for parallel computing, which is becoming increasingly popular. IPython, which you're probably already using as a more convenient interpreter interface, has its own clustering capabilities designed around the ZeroMQ networking system. It can even use MPI on the back end to improve the performance of parallel code. At the moment, not much real-world use of h5py in the IPython parallel model is known to the author. But you should definitely keep an eye on it, if for no other reason than the very convenient interface that IPython provides for clustering.

Threading

HDF5 has no native support for thread-level parallelism. While you can safely use HDF5 (and h5py) from threaded programs, there will be no performance advantage. But for a lot of applications, that's not a problem. GUI apps, for example, spend most of their time waiting for user input.

Before we start, it's important to review a few basics about threaded programming in the Python world. Python itself includes a single master lock that governs access to the interpreter's functions, called the Global Interpreter Lock or GIL. This lock serializes access from multiple threads to basic resources like object reference counting. You can have as many threads as you like in a Python program, but only one at a time can use the interpreter.

This isn't such a big deal, particularly when writing programs like GUIs or web-based applications that spend most of their time waiting for events. In these situations, the GIL is "released" and other threads can use the interpreter while an I/O-bound thread is waiting.

h5py uses a similar concept. Access to HDF5 is serialized using locking, so only one thread at a time can work with the library. Unlike other I/O mechanisms in Python, all use of the HDF5 library is "blocking"; once a call is made to HDF5, the GIL is not released until it completes.

Figure 9-1 shows schematically how this works. If you have multiple threads running, if one of them calls into HDF5 (for example, to write a large dataset to disk), the others will not proceed until the call completes.

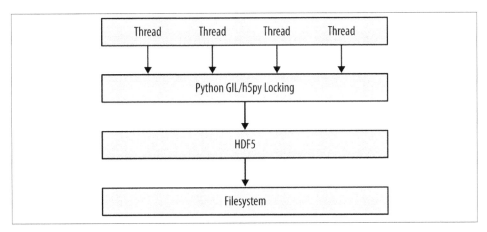

Figure 9-1. Outline of a threading-based program using HDF5

The h5py package is "thread-safe," in that you can safely share objects between threads without corruption, and there's no global state that lets one thread stomp on another. However, certain high-level operations are not yet guaranteed to be atomic. Therefore, it's recommended that you manage access to your HDF5 objects by using recursive locks.

Here's an example: we'll create a single shared HDF5 file and two threads that do some computation and write to it. Access to the file is managed using an instance of the `threading.RLock` class:

```
import threading
import time
import random
import numpy as np
import h5py

f = h5py.File("thread_demo.hdf5", "w")
dset = f.create_dataset("data", (2, 1024), dtype='f')

lock = threading.RLock()

class ComputeThread(threading.Thread):

    def __init__(self, axis):
        self.axis = axis    # One thread does dset[0,:], the other dset[1, :].
        threading.Thread.__init__(self)

    def run(self):
        """ Perform a series of (simulated) computations and save to dataset.
```

```
    """
    for idx in xrange(1024):
        random_number = random.random()*0.01
        time.sleep(random_number)                  # Perform computation
        with lock:
            dset[self.axis, idx] = random_number    # Save to dataset

thread1 = ComputeThread(0)
thread2 = ComputeThread(1)

thread1.start()
thread2.start()

# Wait until both threads have finished
thread1.join()
thread2.join()

f.close()
```

 There's also something out there called "thread-safe" HDF5. This is a compile-time option for the HDF5 library itself. Using it won't hurt anything, but it's not required for thread-safe use of h5py.

Multiprocessing

Because of the GIL, a threading-based Python program can never use more than the equivalent of one processor's time. This is an annoyance when it comes to writing native-Python programs for parallel processing. Historically, people have used ad hoc solutions involving multiple instances of Python, communicating through the filesystem.

Since version 2.6, Python has included an "entry-level" parallel-processing package called multiprocessing. It provides a threading-like way to manage multiple instances of Python.

It is possible to use multiprocessing with HDF5, provided some precautions are taken. The most important thing to remember is that *new processes inherit the state of the HDF5 library from the parent process*. It's very easy to end up in a situation where multiple processes end up "fighting" each other over an open file. At the time of writing (October 2013), this is even true for files that are opened read-only. This has to do with the gory details of how multiprocessing is implemented, using the fork() system call on Linux/Unix operating systems. The HDF Group is aware of this limitation; you should check the most recent documentation for h5py/PyTables to see if it has been resolved.

In the meantime, to avoid problems, here are some things to try:

1. Do all your file I/O in the main process, but don't have files open when you invoke the multiprocessing features.

2. Multiple subprocesses can safely *read* from the same file, but **only open it once the new process has been created.**

3. Have each subprocess *write* to a different file, and merge them when finished.

Figure 9-2 shows workflow (1). The initial process is responsible for file I/O, and communicates with the subprocesses through queues and other multiprocessing constructs.

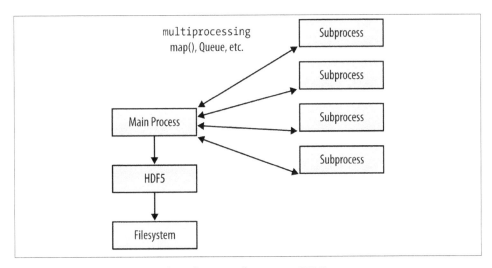

Figure 9-2. Multiprocessing-based approach to using HDF5

One mechanism for "Pythonic" parallel computation is to use "process pools" that distribute the work among worker processes. These are instances of multiprocessing.Pool, which among other things have a parallel equivalent of the built-in map():

```
>>> import string
>>> from multiprocessing import Pool

>>> p = Pool(2)      # Create a 2-process pool

>>> words_in = ['hello', 'some', 'words']
>>> words_out = p.map(string.upper, words_in)
>>> print words_out
['HELLO', 'SOME', 'WORDS']
```

Here's an example of using HDF5 with Pool. Suppose we had a file containing a 1D dataset of coordinate pairs, and we wanted to compute their distance from the origin.

This is the kind of problem that is trivial to parallelize, since each computation doesn't depend on the others. First, we create our file, containing a single coords dataset:

```
with h5py.File('coords.hdf5', 'w') as f:
    dset = f.create_dataset('coords', (1000, 2), dtype='f4')
    dset[...] = np.random.random((1000,2))
```

Our program will use a simple one-liner for the distance measurement, and a four-process Pool to carry out the 1,000 conversions required. Note that we don't have any files open when invoking map:

```
import numpy as np
from multiprocessing import Pool
import h5py

def distance(arr):
    """ Compute distance from origin to the point (arr is a shape-(2,) array)
    """
    return np.sqrt(np.sum(arr**2))

# Load data and close the input file
with h5py.File('coords.hdf5', 'r') as f:
    data = f['coords'][...]

# Create a 4-process pool
p = Pool(4)

# Carry out parallel computation
result = np.array(p.map(distance, data))

# Write the result into a new dataset in the file
with h5py.File('coords.hdf5') as f:
    f['distances'] = result
```

Doing anything more complex with multiprocessing and HDF5 gets complicated. Your processes can't all access the same file. Either you do your I/O explicitly in the main process (as shown), or you have each process generate a bunch of smaller "shard" files and join them together when you're done:

```
import os
import numpy as np
from multiprocessing import Pool
import h5py

def distance_block(idx):
    """ Read a 100-element coordinates block, compute distances, and write
    back out again to a process-specific file.
    """
    with h5py.File('coords.hdf5','r') as f:
        data = f['coords'][idx:idx+100]

    result = np.sqrt(np.sum(data**2, axis=1))
```

```
        with h5py.File('result_index_%d.hdf5'%idx, 'w') as f:
            f['result'] = result

# Create out pool and carry out the computation
p = Pool(4)
p.map(distance_block, xrange(0, 1000, 100))

with h5py.File('coords.hdf5') as f:
    dset = f.create_dataset('distances', (1000,), dtype='f4')

    # Loop over our 100-element "chunks" and merge the data into coords.hdf5
    for idx in xrange(0, 1000, 100):

        filename = 'result_index_%d.hdf5'%idx
        with h5py.File(filename, 'r') as f2:
            data = f2['result'][...]

        dset[idx:idx+100] = data
        os.unlink(filename)  # no longer needed
```

That looks positively exhausting, mainly because of the limitations on passing open files to child processes. What if there were a way to share a single file between processes, automatically synchronizing reads and writes? It turns out there is: Parallel HDF5.

MPI and Parallel HDF5

Figure 9-3 shows how an application works using Parallel HDF5, in contrast to the threading and multiprocessing approaches earlier. MPI-based applications work by launching multiple parallel instances of the Python interpreter. Those instances communicate with each other via the MPI library. The key difference compared to multiprocessing is that the processes are *peers*, unlike the child processes used for the Pool objects we saw earlier.

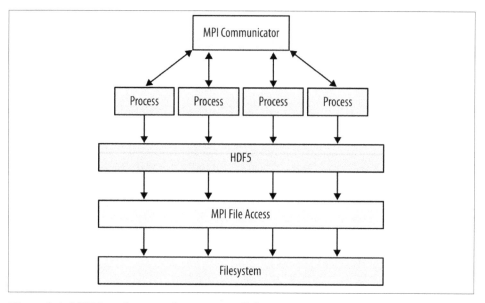

Figure 9-3. MPI-based approach using Parallel HDF5

Of course, this also means that all *file access* has to be coordinated though the MPI library as well. If not, multiple processes would "fight" over the same file on disk. Thankfully, HDF5 itself handles nearly all the details involved with this. All you need to do is open shared files with a special driver, and follow some constraints for data consistency.

Let's take a look at how MPI-based programs work in Python before diving into Parallel HDF5.

A Very Quick Introduction to MPI

MPI-based programs work a little differently from thread-based or `multiprocessing` programs. Since there's no explicit creation of processes on the Python side, you write a Python script and launch it with the special program `mpiexec`. Here's the "Hello World" example for MPI:

```
from mpi4py import MPI

comm = MPI.COMM_WORLD

print "Hello World (from process %d)" % comm.rank
```

To run it with four processes, we launch Python via `mpiexec`:

```
$ mpiexec -n 4 python demo.py
Hello World (from process 0)
Hello World (from process 1)
```

```
Hello World (from process 3)
Hello World (from process 2)
```

The COMM_WORLD object is an MPI *communicator*. Communication between processes all happens though the MPI library, via these objects. In addition to "send" and "receive" methods, communicators in MPI support a variety of advanced "scatter" operations to distribute work among processes. Since a complete treatment of MPI features is beyond the scope of this book, we will limit ourselves to a few basic features.

The COMM_WORLD attribute rank is an integer that identifies the running process. You'll notice that the output statements print "out of order" with respect to rank. As with threads, since our four processes run in parallel there's no guarantee as to which will finish first. Later on we'll examine some basic methods for interprocess synchronization.

Check out the mpi4py website (*http://mpi4py.scipy.org*) for a great introduction to using MPI from Python, and a large number of examples.

MPI-Based HDF5 Program

Building h5py in MPI mode is simple. The tricky bit is getting access to a version of HDF5 compiled in "parallel" mode; increasingly, this is available as a built-in package on most Linux distributions. Then, when you build h5py, just enable the --mpi option:

```
$ python setup.py build --mpi [--hdf5=/path/to/parallel/hdf5]
$ [sudo] python setup.py install
```

If you have installation problems, consult the guide at www.h5py.org for tips and additional examples. The examples shown here use an OpenMPI build of HDF5, running on Linux.

On the Python side, all you have to do is open your file with the mpio driver. You have to supply an MPI communicator as well; COMM_WORLD does nicely:

```
from mpi4py import MPI
import h5py

f = h5py.File("foo.hdf5", "w", driver="mpio", comm=MPI.COMM_WORLD)
```

In contrast to the other file drivers, a file opened with mpio can safely be accessed from multiple processes.

Here's the MPI equivalent of our distance-calculation code. Note that the division of work is done *implicitly* (in this case using the process rank) in contrast to the explicit map()-based approach we saw in the multiprocessing example:

```
import numpy as np
import h5py
from mpi4py import MPI

comm = MPI.COMM_WORLD    # Communicator which links all our processes together
rank = comm.rank         # Number which identifies this process.  Since we'll
                         # have 4 processes, this will be in the range 0-3.

f = h5py.File('coords.hdf5', driver='mpio', comm=comm)

coords_dset = f['coords']
distances_dset = f.create_dataset('distances', (1000,), dtype='f4')

idx = rank*250  # This will be our starting index.  Rank 0 handles coordinate
                # pairs 0-249, Rank 1 handles 250-499, Rank 2 500-749, and
                # Rank 3 handles 750-999.

coords = coords_dset[idx:idx+250]  # Load process-specific data

result = np.sqrt(np.sum(coords**2, axis=1))  # Compute distances

distances_dset[idx:idx+250] = result  # Write process-specific data

f.close()
```

Collective Versus Independent Operations

MPI has two flavors of operation: *collective*, which means that all processes have to participate (and in the same order), and *independent*, which means each process can perform the operation (or not) whenever and in whatever order it pleases.

With HDF5, the main requirement is this: *modifications to file metadata must be done collectively*. Here are some things that qualify:

- Opening or closing a file
- Creating or deleting new datasets, groups, attributes, or named types
- Changing a dataset's shape
- Moving or copying objects in the file

Generally this isn't a big deal. What it means for your code is the following: when you're executing different code paths depending on the process rank (or as the result of an interprocess communication), make sure you stick to data I/O only. In contrast to metadata operations, data operations (meaning reading from and writing to existing HDF5) are OK for processes to perform independently.

Here are some simple examples:

```
from mpi4py import MPI
import h5py
```

```
comm = MPI.COMM_WORLD
rank = comm.rank

f = h5py.File('collective_test.hdf5', 'w', driver='mpio', comm=comm)

# RIGHT: All processes participate when creating an object
dset = f.create_dataset('x', (100,), 'i')

# WRONG: Only one process participating in a metadata operation
if rank == 0:
    dset.attrs['title'] = "Hello"

# RIGHT: Data I/O can be independent
if rank == 0:
    dset[0] = 42

# WRONG: All processes must participate in the same order
if rank == 0:
    f.attrs['a'] = 10
    f.attrs['b'] = 20
else:
    f.attrs['b'] = 20
    f.attrs['a'] = 10
```

When you violate this requirement, generally you *won't* get an exception; instead, various Bad Things will happen behind the scenes, possibly endangering your data.

Note that "collective" does *not* mean "synchronized." Although all processes in the preceding example call `create_dataset`, for example, they don't pause until the others catch up. The only requirements are that every process has to make the call, and in the same order.

Atomicity Gotchas

Sometimes, it's necessary to synchronize the state of multiple processes. For example, you might want to ensure that the first stage of a distributed calculation is finished before moving on to the next part. MPI provides a number of mechanisms to deal with this. The simplest is called "barrier synchronization"—from the Python side, this is simply a function called `Barrier` that blocks until every process has reached the same point in the program.

Here's an example. This program generally prints "A" and "B" statements out of order:

```
from random import random
from time import sleep
from mpi4py import MPI

comm = MPI.COMM_WORLD
rank = comm.rank
```

```
    sleep(random()*5)
    print "A (rank %d)" % rank
    sleep(random()*5)
    print "B (rank %d)" % rank
```

Running it, we get:

```
$ mpiexec -n 4 python demo2.py
A (rank 2)
B (rank 2)
A (rank 1)
A (rank 0)
B (rank 1)
A (rank 3)
B (rank 3)
B (rank 0)
```

Our COMM_WORLD communicator includes a Barrier function. If we add a barrier for all processes just before the "B" print statement, we get:

```
from random import random
from time import sleep
from mpi4py import MPI

comm = MPI.COMM_WORLD
rank = comm.rank

sleep(random()*5)
print "A (rank %d)" % rank

comm.Barrier()  # Blocks until all processes catch up

sleep(random()*5)
print "B (rank %d)" % rank

$ mpiexec -n 4 python demo3.py
A (rank 2)
A (rank 3)
A (rank 0)
A (rank 1)
B (rank 2)
B (rank 0)
B (rank 1)
B (rank 3)
```

Now that you know about Barrier, what do you think the following two-process program outputs?

```
import h5py
from mpi4py import MPI

comm = MPI.COMM_WORLD
rank = comm.rank
```

```
with h5py.File('atomicdemo.hdf5', 'w', driver='mpio', comm=comm) as f:

    dset = f.create_dataset('x', (1,), dtype='i')

    if rank == 0:
        dset[0] = 42

    comm.Barrier()

    if rank == 1:
        print dset[0]
```

If you answered "42," you're *wrong*. You might get 42, and you might get 0. This is one of the most irritating things about MPI from a consistency standpoint. The default write semantics do not guarantee that writes will have completed before `Barrier` returns and the program moves on. Why? Performance. Since MPI is typically used for huge, thousand-processor problems, people are willing to put up with relaxed consistency requirements to get every last bit of speed possible.

Starting with HDF5 1.8.9, there is a feature to get around this. You can enable MPI "atomic" mode for your file. This turns on a low-level feature that trades performance for strict consistency requirements. Among other things, it means that `Barrier` (and other MPI synchronization methods) interact with writes the way you expect. This modified program will always print "42":

```
import h5py
from mpi4py import MPI

comm = MPI.COMM_WORLD
rank = comm.rank

with h5py.File('atomicdemo.hdf5', 'w', driver='mpio', comm=comm) as f:

    f.atomic = True  # Enables strict atomic mode (requires HDF5 1.8.9+)

    dset = f.create_dataset('x', (1,), dtype='i')

    if rank == 0:
        dset[0] = 42

    comm.Barrier()

    if rank == 1:
        print dset[0]
```

The trade-off, of course, is reduced performance. Generally the best solution is to avoid passing data from process to process through the file. MPI has great interprocess communication tools. Use them!

## CHAPTER 10

Next Steps

Now that you have a firm introduction to HDF5, it's up to you to put that knowledge to use! Here are some resources to help you on your way.

Asking for Help

The Python community is very open, and this extends to users of h5py, NumPy, and SciPy. Don't be afraid to ask for help on the h5py (*h5py@googlegroups.com*), NumPy (*numpy-discussions@scipy.org*), or SciPy (*scipy-user@scipy.org*) mailing lists. Stack Overflow (*http://stackoverflow.com*) is also a great place to ask specific technical questions if you're getting started with the NumPy world.

You can find technical documentation for h5py, including API reference material, at www.h5py.org. The HDF Group's website (*http://www.hdfgroup.org*) also has an extensive reference manual and user guide (from a C programmer's perspective).

If you're working on an "application" of HDF5, like EOS5, get in touch with that community for more information on how files are structured. For general questions on HDF5 (as opposed to h5py or Python), you can post to the HDF Group's public forum at *hdf-forum@lists.hdfgroup.org*. The HDF Group can also be reached directly for bug reports, technical questions, and so on at *help@hdfgroup.org*.

Finally, if you're craving more information on using Python for scientific coding, *Python for Data Analysis* (McKinney, 2012) is a great place to start. Tutorials and reference materials are also available on the SciPy website (*http://scipy.org*) for those seeking a quick introduction to analysis in Python, or just looking for the `fft` function.

Contributing

As you continue to use HDF5, you may occasionally have a bug to report or a feature request. Both the h5py (*http://github.com/h5py/h5py*) and PyTables (*http://github.com/*

PyTables/PyTables) projects are on GitHub and welcome user bug reports and features. Using the `git` revision control system and GitHub's "pull requests" feature, you can even contribute code directly to the projects. Read more about how to contribute at www.h5py.org.

Index

We'd like to hear your suggestions for improving our indexes. Send email to index@oreilly.com.

root, 55
storage of, 65
sub-, 55
widgets for, 57
GZIP compression, 50

H

h5py documentation, 127
h5repack tool, 59
half-precision floats, 88
hard links, 57–59
soft links vs., 59
hard-linking objects, 64
hashing, 72
HDF command-line tools, 15
HDF group, 109, 127
HDF5, 1–8
application formating over, 82–84
contributing to, 127
datasets, 5
Dimension Scales specification, 109
ecosystem, 6
endinaness and, 35
file object, 17–20
filters for, 50
h5py package (Python), 11
Image standard, 109
libraries for, 6
main elements, 5
multiprocessing and, 116
Parallel, 19
Python and, 2–4
SQL relational databases vs., 5
thread-safe, 116
tools for, 14–17
types in, 87
visitor feature, 13
HDFView, 14
hierarchically organized groups, 2

I

identifiers, 72
Image standard, 109
image tiles, 43
independent operations (MPI), 122
indexing
boolean, 31
expressions, 32

fancy, 33
fancy, and region references, 105
groups, 7
start-stop-step, 29
indices
fastest-varying, 42
NumPy vs., 29
optional, 66
inspecting files, 14
integers, 87
converting enumerated types to, 96
internal data structures, 7
international characters, 62
IPython module (Python), 11, 21, 114
clustering with, 114
ISO format, 99
iteration, 62, 65–68
canceling, 70
dictionary-style, 66
groups and, 67
methods, 66
multilevel, 68–71
visitor, 68–71

L

links, 57–65
external, 61
free space and, 59
get method and, 63
hard, 57–59
object names and, 62
object types, determining, 63
references vs., 102
repacking and, 59
require method and, 64
soft, 59–61
storing as data, 102
to named types, 107
types of, 64
Linux, 11
list-based selections, 106
little-endian format, 1, 35, 88
big-endian format vs., 1
LZF compression, 51

M

mailing lists, 127
masks, 31

dense, 78
filters, 48–54
hashing, 72
iteration, 65–68
objects, copying, 71
storing numerical data, 2
strides, 10, 42
string flavor, 81, 91
strings
    byte vs. Unicode, 91
    fixed-length, 89
    in Python 2, 93
    limits of, 90
    storing binary data in, 93
    types of, 89
    variable-length, 89–93
structured arrays, 94
subselections, 32
subsetting I/O, 4
SZIP compression, 50

T

text strings, 62, 92
    attributes and, 76
    byte strings into, 92
    byte strings vs., 79
    visitor iteration and, 69
thread-level parallelism, 114
thread-safe package, 115
threading, 114–116
threads, 113
time types, 99
timeit module (Python), 12
tools (HDF5), 14–17
    command line, 15
    HDFView, 14
    ViTables, 15
tracking free space, 59
trimming datasets, 39
type conversion, 24
types, 87–100
    array, 97
    attributes and, 77
    automatic conversion, 24
    Boolean, 96
    complex numbers, 95
    compound, 93–95
    date, 99
    endinaness and, 35

    enumerated, 95
    explicit, 80–82
    fixed-length strings, 89
    floats, 88
    in HDF5, 87
    integers, 88
    named, 106–108
    of file compatibility, 78
    opaque, 98
    Python objects, 78
    time, 99
    variable-length strings, 89–93

U

Unicode
    characters, 92
    filenames, 17
Unicode strings, 79, 91
    fixed-width, 89
    in Python, 92
    wide-character, 89
Unix time, 99
unlimited axes, 37
unsigned integers, 88
updating datasets, 32
user block (file object), 19
user-defined metadata attributes, 2

V

variable-length strings, 79, 90
    vlen data type, 90
variable-sized steps, 109
visit items method, 70
visitor iteration, 68–71
    by name, 68
    multiple links and, 69
    text strings and, 69
    visit items method and, 70
visitor pattern, 69
ViTables, 15

W

wide-character Unicode strings, 89
wrappers, 11
write_direct method, 35
writing files, 6
writing to datasets, 27

About the Author

Andrew Collette holds a Ph.D. in physics from UCLA and works as a laboratory research scientist at the University of Colorado. He has worked with the Python-NumPy-HDF5 stack at two multimillion-dollar research facilities, the first being the Large Plasma Device at UCLA (entirely standardized on HDF5), and the second being the hypervelocity dust accelerator at the Colorado Center for Lunar Dust and Atmospheric Studies, University of Colorado at Boulder. Additionally, Dr. Collette is a leading developer of the HDF5 for Python (h5py) project.

Colophon

The animals on the cover of *Python and HDF5* are parrot crossbills (*Loxia pytyopsittacus*). Rather than being related to parrots in any way, the parrot crossbill is actually a species of finch that lives in northwestern Europe and western Russia. There is also a small population in Scotland, where it is difficult to distinguish the parrot from the related red and Scottish Crossbills. The parrot crossbill's name comes from the fact that the upper mandible overlaps the lower one, giving it the same shape as many parrots' beaks. This adaptation makes it easy for the birds to extract seeds from conifer cones, which are their main source of food. In Scotland, they are specialist feeders on the cones of the Scots pine. It is very difficult to tell parrot crossbills apart from the other species of Loxia, but there are a few clues. Parrot crossbills are slightly bigger, have the curved beak, and have a deeper call than the others. They also tend to have a bigger head. All three species share the same territory and breeding range; the males are reddish orange in color, while the females are olive green or gray. On average, a female will have a clutch of three or four eggs, which she incubates for about two weeks. Once the chicks have hatched, they live in the nest for about a month before starting out on their own. Due to its large geographic range and stable population numbers, the Parrot Crossbill is not considered endangered or threatened in any way.

The cover images are from Wood's *Animate Creation*. The cover fonts are URW Typewriter and Guardian Sans. The text font is Adobe Minion Pro; the heading font is Adobe Myriad Condensed; and the code font is Dalton Maag's Ubuntu Mono.

Get even more for your money.

Join the O'Reilly Community, and register the O'Reilly books you own. It's free, and you'll get:

- $4.99 ebook upgrade offer
- 40% upgrade offer on O'Reilly print books
- Membership discounts on books and events
- Free lifetime updates to ebooks and videos
- Multiple ebook formats, DRM FREE
- Participation in the O'Reilly community
- Newsletters
- Account management
- 100% Satisfaction Guarantee

Signing up is easy:

1. **Go to: oreilly.com/go/register**
2. **Create an O'Reilly login.**
3. **Provide your address.**
4. **Register your books.**

Note: English-language books only

To order books online:
oreilly.com/store

For questions about products or an order:
orders@oreilly.com

To sign up to get topic-specific email announcements and/or news about upcoming books, conferences, special offers, and new technologies:
elists@oreilly.com

For technical questions about book content:
booktech@oreilly.com

To submit new book proposals to our editors:
proposals@oreilly.com

O'Reilly books are available in multiple DRM-free ebook formats. For more information:
oreilly.com/ebooks

Spreading the knowledge of innovators   oreilly.com

Milton Keynes UK
Ingram Content Group UK Ltd.
UKHW011008260724
446093UK00007B/143